- Inspirations From Eastern England Vol II

Edited by Steve Twelvetree

Young**Writers**
First published in Great Britain in 2005 by:
Young Writers
Remus House
Coltsfoot Drive
Peterborough
PE2 9JX
Telephone: 01733 890066
Website: www.youngwriters.co.uk

All Rights Reserved

© *Copyright Contributors 2005*

SB ISBN 1 84602 261 4

Foreword

Young Writers was established in 1991 and has been passionately devoted to the promotion of reading and writing in children and young adults ever since. The quest continues today. Young Writers remains as committed to the fostering of burgeoning poetic and literary talent as ever.

This year's Young Writers competition has proven as vibrant and dynamic as ever and we are delighted to present a showcase of the best poetry from across the UK. Each poem has been carefully selected from a wealth of *Playground Poets* entries before ultimately being published in this, our thirteenth primary school poetry series.

Once again, we have been supremely impressed by the overall high quality of the entries we have received. The imagination, energy and creativity which has gone into each young writer's entry made choosing the best poems a challenging and often difficult but ultimately hugely rewarding task - the general high standard of the work submitted amply vindicating this opportunity to bring their poetry to a larger appreciative audience.

We sincerely hope you are pleased with our final selection and that you will enjoy *Playground Poets - Inspirations From Eastern England Vol II* for many years to come.

Contents

Benhurst Primary School, Hornchurch
Ugo Nwangwu (8)	1
Onyinyechi Ihedioha (9)	2
Jade McCarthy (8)	3
George Dines (8)	4
Daisy Cumming (8)	4
Emily Morgan (9)	5
Elizabeth Fisher (8)	5
Jamie Ash (7)	6
Davita Lamai (8)	6
Alice Peppard (9)	7
Emmanuel Awoniyi (8)	7
Annie Stoneman (7)	8
Molly Bryan (8)	9
Harry Stoneman (9)	10
Frankie Phillips (8)	10
Jessie Butler (7)	11
Victor Awoniyi (9)	11
Danielle Khick (8)	12
Ajibola Lawal (9)	12
Katie Hunt (8)	13
Gabrielle Woodward (8)	13
Louisa Beckwith (9)	14
Hannah Barker (9)	15

Blenheim Park Community Primary School, Fakenham
Nathaniel Newman (11)	15
Abbie Charlton (11)	16
Emma Weller (11)	16
Jacob Holland (10)	16
Bryony Newstead (11)	17
Alysha Childs (11)	17
Hannah Hewitt (10)	17
Rosie Hewitt (11)	18
Jake Battrick (11)	18

Chigwell Primary School, Chigwell
Liam Hall (10)	19

Cleveland Junior School, Ilford
Ibrahim Inayat (8)	20
Neera Senthivel (8)	20
Tobi Akinola (7)	21
Humza Mehmood (7)	21
Mohamed Abdulkarim (8)	22
Aaron Dha (8)	22
Zainab Maqbool (8)	22
Ikra Ali (8)	23
Vinit Vikuntam (8)	23
Emran Ali (7)	23
Sahra Mohamed (8)	24
Leila Jassal (8)	24
Ankit Patel (8)	25
Mithilaa Senthivel (8)	25
Evandra Paulo (8)	26
Iqra Masood (8)	26
Uniza Zia (8)	27

Doggetts CP School, Rochford
Gemma Reed (11)	27
Bethany Ellaway (10)	28
Becky Roper (8)	28
Jessica Lambert (11)	29
Olivia Spearman (8)	29
Emily Davis (9)	30
Abby Hare (7)	30
Rebecca Ramsey (10)	31
Callum Soper (10)	31
Kris Neave-Houghting (11)	32
Jade Lewin (10)	32
Louis Cash (10)	33
Peter Currell (8)	33
Dean Eagle (11)	33
Megan Loker (8)	34
Lily Humpage (11)	35
Iona Walkling (9)	36
Chloe Newcombe (9)	36

Dycorts Special School, Romford
Glen Atkin (10)	36
Harry Thomas (10)	37
Joe Fordham (10)	37
Billy Isham (10)	37

East Winch CE (VA) Primary School, King's Lynn
Georgina Power (11)	38
Chelsea Palmer (10)	38
Haley Knowles (12)	39
Matthew Atkin (10)	39
Amy Cross (7)	40
Alex Parkinson (11)	40
Thomas Bailey (8)	40
Perry Large (11)	41
Laura Wilson (9)	41
Emily Gooding (8)	41

Eversley Primary School, Basildon
Ellie-Jo Hodgson (11)	42
Lacey Brooks (11)	42
Benjamin Robinson (10)	43
Holly Philpot (11)	43
Jack Dickinson (11)	43
Charlotte Nicholls (10)	44
Jake Batten (11)	44

Harleston CE (VA) Primary School
Samantha Reeve (11)	45
Amy Leeder (10)	45
Rhian Earrye (11)	46
Stephanie Knox (11)	46
Sinead Carey (11)	47
Andrew Langham-Service (11)	47
Devon Green (10)	47
Douglas Webber (11)	48
Jack Lovick (11)	48
Danielle Hines (11)	48
Matthew Buchan (11)	49
Kyle Kenneally (11)	49

Vicki Scofield (11)	50
Alex Burlton (10)	50
Isabel Cockle (11)	51
Charlie Oakes (10)	51
Danielle O'Connor (10)	51
Joe Collins (10)	52
James Baker (11)	52
Bronwyn Elsden (11)	52
Kane Peacock (11)	53
Emma Jackson (11)	53
Rory James (11)	53
Emma Earye (11)	54

John Bunyan Junior School, Braintree

Luke Bellingham (10)	54
Steven Wheeler (11)	55
Caleb Wicker (8)	55
Ryan Harris (11)	56
Kelvin Chuttur (10)	56
Amy Spooner (11)	57
Tyler Duchar-Clark (10)	57
Thomas Ranson (10)	58
Beth Pasfield (9)	58
Ben Wiseman (8)	58
Colbran Tokley (11)	59
Cornelius O'Leary (11)	59
David Roberts (11)	60
Rebecca Pitcher (10)	60
Amber Clarey (9)	61
Danielle Read (9)	61
Jorden Stedman (8)	62
Lynsey Colbert (8)	62
Drew Rogers (8)	63
Natalie Butler (11)	63
I'esha Lewin (8)	64
Sophie Clark (9)	64
Ben Nichols (9)	65

John Ray Junior School, Braintree

Sydnee Collins (8)	65
Lauren Wiffen (8)	65

Aaron Benfield (8)	66
Portia Boehmer (8)	66
Molly Poulton (8)	66
Charlotte Hughes (8)	67
Gabriella Mackay (8)	67
Thomas Jarman (8)	67
Lauren Chambers (8)	68
Shannon Gates (8)	68
Eren Tokkan (8)	68
Charlotte Willett (8)	69
Sean Keeling (7)	69
Charlotte Rossiter (7)	69
James Best (7)	70
Rebecca Elsey (8)	70
Jordan Pannell (8)	70

Morland Primary School, Ipswich

Charlotte McNamara (10)	71
Kira Wymer (10)	72
Rochelle Rankin (9)	72
Jasmine Fairs (10)	73
Leanne Goldsmith (9)	73
Jennifer Mok (10)	74
Adam Keevil (10)	74
Amena Ali (9)	75
Josh McNamee (10)	75
Brady Todd (10)	76
Curtis Saunders (9)	77
Bethany Mortimer (9)	77
Grant Day (9)	78

Newtons Primary School, Rainham

Jack Burke (8)	78
Maherban Lidher (11)	79
Abbie Wyatt (8)	79
Jessica Palmer (11)	80
Shanyce Duffy (8)	80
Jessie Kivuitu (9)	81
Jordan Nastri (10)	81
Maria Rolfe (10)	82
Daniel Small (10)	82

Jennifer Harrad (9)	82
Shannon Hemsley (9)	83
Charlie Davis (10)	83
Jack Watson (10)	83
Jade Scanlan (9)	84
Joanna Annett (10)	84
Ruth Adediran (9)	84
Hayley East (10)	85
Claire Potts (10)	85
Sophie Barton (9)	85
Georgina Poulton (10)	86
Sophie Walker	86
Chelsea McDiarmaid (10)	86
Harry Nolan (10)	87
Daisy Young (10)	87
Alexandra Grace (11)	87
Elliot Scott (11)	88
Jai Small (11)	88
Jack Mercer (10)	89
Frazer Collins (11)	89
James Cartwright (9)	90
Katie Wong (11)	90
Luke Scott (11)	91
Jordan Collins (11)	91
Albert Sherwood (11)	92
Chelsey Chase (11)	92
Kastriot Memeti (11)	93
Jade Gale (11)	93
Rinna Ernstzen (8)	94
Chantel Dyer (11)	94
Nancy Foley-Gannon (11)	95
Jade Pattison (11)	95
Kane Robertson (10)	96
Roseline Mgbeike (11)	96
Aaron Howard (8)	96
Taryn Harley (9)	97
Georgia Cunningham (10)	97
Gregoria Gati (8)	98
Taylor Thacker (8)	98
Shannon Davis (9)	99
Risan Nishori (8)	99
Toby Cox (9)	99

Celine Franklin (9)	100
Charlotte Coleman (9)	100
Ashlie East (8)	101
Liam Renham (9)	101
Peace Ugbeikwu (9)	102
Dafina Nishori (9)	102
Lauren Smith (10)	103
Jack Kennedy (9)	103
Joseph Hatcher (8)	103
Nicole Painter (9)	104
Jay Wyatt (10)	104

Rainham Village Primary School, Rainham

Jack Ogbourne (11)	104
Nicole Gregory (10)	105
Sam Harber (11)	105
Daisy Cook (11)	106
Abbie Carter (9)	106
Dean Brunt (8)	107
Samantha Sommerville (8)	107
Annie Boxer (9)	108
Arron Bernard (9)	108
Sarah Aramide (11)	109
Tyler Roberts (9)	109
Charles Hall (10)	110
Katie Nelson (9)	110
Robert Park (10)	111
Aliyah Park (7)	111
Michael Busby (10)	112
John Beth (11)	112
Zoe Elsmore (10)	113
Stephanie Lovett (10)	113
Abiola Ricketts (10)	114
Olivia Ibanez-Solano (11)	114
Kirsty Lake (11)	115
Joseph Smyth (8)	115
Joanne Price (10)	116
Samuel Wood (8)	116
Lucy Ramsey (8)	117
Robert-Lee Hall (8)	117
Danielle Beavis (8)	118

Elizabeth Miller (10)	118
Deanna Gammans (9)	119
Christopher Thompson (10)	119
Joanna Guzman (10)	120
Jasleen Bhogal (11)	120
Teal Anderson (10)	121
Jasdeep Nijjar (8)	122
Hayley Kitt (10)	122
Sarah Beeson (10)	122
Fatmata Jah (10)	123
Sarah Skipper (11)	123
Adam Challis (11)	124
Thomas Tyrrell (11)	124
Katherine Rodwell (11)	125
Philip Modu (10)	125
Chloe Hemmett Fuller (9)	126
Lynsey Coleman (11)	126
James Lofty (10)	127
Katherine Wisbey (11)	127
Jonathan Hime (10)	128
Nikita Ghataura (8)	128
Gareth Beth (9)	129
Michael Olaribigbe (10)	129
Lauren Ginn (10)	130
Scott Coghlan (8)	130
Melissa Hunt (9)	131
Emma McCloud (9)	131
Kayleigh Saunter (9)	132
Marvyn Ashton (10)	132
Awais Butt (10)	133
Kelly Mavididi (9)	134
Amie Cook (8)	134
Zachary Pearce (9)	135

Riverside Middle School, Mildenhall

Kayla Nielsen (11)	135
Oliver Smith (10)	135
Harry Clark (9)	136
Keyarno Curtis (9)	136
Melissa Jackson (10)	136
Joshua Feltner (9)	137

Luke Ames (10)	137
Chris Barton (10)	137
Curtis Cronin (10)	138
Harry Leonard (9)	138
Edward Pooley (9)	138
Sam Davis (10)	138
Martin Shaw (10)	139
Keturah Cumber (10)	139
Jay Sharp (10)	139
Charlotte Baker (9)	140
Elliott Langham (10)	140
Amy Flack (10)	140
Haleigh Bragg (9)	140
Alex Goodenough (10)	141
Ashleigh Tilbrook (10)	141
Sean Hebb (10)	141

Rose Hill Primary School, Ipswich

Leah Patterson (8)	141
Louise Harling (7)	142
George Bemrose (7)	142
Kai Hardy (7)	142
Esther Howard (7)	143
Harrison Smith (7)	143
Benjamin Kersey (7)	143
Conor Sparkes (7)	144
Emily Jones (9)	144
Courtney Pattison (9)	144
Khyle Phillips (10)	145
Luke Johnson (8)	145
Daniel Garnham (7)	145
Mahalia Griffin (10)	146
Alex Keinzley (9)	146
Jade Nunn (8)	147
Jozef Ochwat (7)	147
Luke Howard (9)	148
Aidan Bull (9)	148
Abigail Eaton (10)	149
Benjamin Golding (9)	149
Emily O'Neill (10)	150
Gianni Lesina (8)	150

Jenny Hardwicke (11)	151
Jessica Delaney (8)	151
Ellen Wootten (9)	152
Danielle Fulcher (9)	152
Lydia Grant (9)	153
Joshua Keeble (10)	153
Callum Sparkes (9)	154
Ellie Sampson (8)	154
Emily Kenny (10)	155
Nichola Sapsed (10)	155
Madison Nunn (11)	156
Alexandra Kell (11)	156
Bethany Exworth (10)	157

Rudham CE Primary School, King's Lynn

Timothy Florax (10)	157
Charlotte Maloney Parr-Burman (6)	158
Archie Cross (7)	158
Danielle Meyern (8)	159
Bradley White (8)	159
Eleanor Maloney Parr-Burman (8)	160
Holly Page (10)	160
Heather McKinnon (9)	161
Cally Haclin (9)	161
Luke Henson (9)	162
Georgina Meyern (9)	163
Josie Henson (11)	164
Michaela Pitkin-Bovington (9)	165
Lizzie Prentis (11)	166
Jamie Thompson (11)	166
Thomas Hill (8)	167
Fleur Murphy (8)	167
Jack McCarthy (10)	168

St Margaret's CE Primary School, Halstead

Ryan Hatton (10)	168
Hannah Pyman (10)	169
Connie James (11)	169
Sasha Osborn (10)	170
Iszak Smith (9)	170

Amelia Quinn (11)	171
Lauren Platt (9)	171

St Philip's Priory School, Chelmsford
Farwa Jeddy (10)	172
Alexander Read (8)	172
Elysia Booker (10)	173
Samuel Taylor Burns (8)	173
Edward Lakin (10)	174
Cara Chan (8)	174
Chengetai Chirewa (10)	175
Max Purkiss (8)	175
Hester Catchpole (10)	176
Maham Qureshi (8)	176
Sam Purkiss (10)	177
Megan Larner-Hoskins (8)	177
Rosanna Beaver (9)	178
Erin Lucid (9)	178
Sophie Lampshire (10)	179
Nadia Wheadon (10)	180
Hallam Dyckhoff (10)	181
Elena Impieri (10)	182
Will Adams (8)	182
Ridhae Sheikh (10)	183
Francesca Impieri (8)	183
Sam Davis (10)	184
Danielle Tinloi (10)	185
Katie Lampshire (8)	185
Jessica Jellicoe (10)	186
Francesca Read (8)	186
Nelia Leong (8)	187

Salhouse Primary School, Norwich
Vanessa Allen (7)	187
Sophie Thurling (7)	188
Grady Patten (7)	188

Tilney St Lawrence CP School, Tilney St Lawrence
Sarah Papworth (11)	188

Westwood Primary School, Benfleet
Helena Bonici (11)   189
Thomas Haylock (8)   189
Thomas Clubb (8)   189
Andrew Brown (11)   190
George Hughes (10)   190
Chloe Harman (10)   191
Heather Wilson (9)   191

The Poems

The Dragon Of China

It rises in night and sets at dawn
The dragon of China,
Punishes everyone that breaks the law
The dragon of China.

It's red and blue and it's coming for food
The dragon of China.
It's not always in a good mood
The dragon of China.

It rides along the windy sky,
The dragon of China,
Never ever lie in the dragon of China's sight
The dragon of China.

It's ripped and torn in a toy box
So what is this fascinating dragon of China?
It's stuffed with fluff
And squashy stuff.

I take him to bed every day
It's ripped and torn but I love him anyway.
The dragon of China
He's better than hugging a teddy bear.

Being the owner of
The dragon of China
It's stuffed with fluff and squashy stuff
That's why I like him the most.

Ugo Nwangwu (8)
Benhurst Primary School, Hornchurch

Friends 4 Ever

I have a friend
Called Orika

She follows me
Everywhere I go

I went to the
Cinema one day

She brought
Some sweets

And I brought
Some too

I follow her
She follows me

We play
About

We act
About

We hang
Around

We sing
About

But most of all we're friends forever.

Onyinyechi Ihedioha (9)
Benhurst Primary School, Hornchurch

What I Do!

I went to shop
And bought a top
And then bought a lollipop.

I went to bed
And my Ted
Goodnight my mum said.

Get up you've got to go to school
And be cool
Then jump in the pool.

I'm having fun
I had a bun
Then saw the sun.

I found a tin
I looked for a bin
And then went in.

I saw a star
And had a bar
I said I won't go far.

I saw the moon
And stayed up till dawn
And then I went to find corn.

Jade McCarthy (8)
Benhurst Primary School, Hornchurch

Henry VIII

I am Henry, fat and slow
I ride on a motorbike and off I go
I eat, I drink, all I wish
For I am the King of England.

I pick my nose
And stretch my toes
But I don't care
Because I am the King of England.

I snore right loud
Above the clouds
Whoever hears I don't care
Because I am the King of England.

I smell under arms and legs
Sometimes I wish I had pegs,
I never flush the chain, it must get smelly

        For I am the King of England.

George Dines (8)
Benhurst Primary School, Hornchurch

My First Day At Brownies

It's my first day at Brownies
What should I wear?

It's my first day at Brownies
Is there a girl called Claire?

What are the girls' names?
How do I get there?
What do I do?

But let's not worry,
I've got my friend Molly,
Then after I can have a lovely lolly.

Daisy Cumming (8)
Benhurst Primary School, Hornchurch

Animals

There was a dog
Who was furry
There was a cat
Who was purry
There was a fish who was swimming
In the pond.

There was a tiny hamster
Eating cheese
There was a slow tortoise
Walking on the grass.

There was a dirty dog rolling in the mud
There was a cat
Purring on the grass.

Emily Morgan (9)
Benhurst Primary School, Hornchurch

Nonsense Poem

One day I went to New York
I went to Burger King and had a dish of pork
An elephant came wandering in
I was so scared I hid in a tin.

Now six years have gone, it's in the past
I think it has gone really fast
Now I think I should have stayed
I really shouldn't really have paid.

Don't forget, don't go to New York
And have a dish of pork.

Elizabeth Fisher (8)
Benhurst Primary School, Hornchurch

The Jungle

In the jungle
There's a lion
Creeping up on everyone
That sleeps through the day and on.

In the jungle,
There's a monkey
Swinging in the trees,
Eating bananas that are chunky.

In the jungle,
There's a crocodile
Snapping its jaws
Waiting for a while.

In the jungle,
There's a tiger,
Prowling about,
Hiding from a sniper.

In the jungle,
There's an alligator,
Swimming about,
Near a crater.

Jamie Ash (7)
Benhurst Primary School, Hornchurch

Here Is A Song

Here is a song that you probably don't know.
Here is a chair that you don't sit on.
Here is a fire that you don't light.
Here is a battle that you don't fight.
Here is a bed that you don't sleep on.
Here is a class that you don't teach.
Here is a wig you do not wear.
      That is ungratefulness!

Davita Lamai (8)
Benhurst Primary School, Hornchurch

Cats

Cats miaow
While they sit on a towel
And they sit proudly
In the lounge.

Cats scratch all day long
While they sing a little song
When they get home they have tea,
Then they go out again.

Cats miaow
While they sit on a towel
And they sit proudly
In the lounge.

Cats are all different colours
They are excellent at running
When they go to bed,
They dream all different things.

Cats miaow
While they sit on a towel
And sits proudly
In the lounge.

Alice Peppard (9)
Benhurst Primary School, Hornchurch

My Friend

My friend is really bad
He makes me really sad
He makes me chew his shoe
While he's playing pranks with his friend Barry in the loo
He made me be a queen
And he was really mean
He made me eat chips
And he made me give him chocolate dips.

Emmanuel Awoniyi (8)
Benhurst Primary School, Hornchurch

I Went To The Animal Zoo

I went to the animal zoo
I wanted to go with you
I saw a fat monkey
My mum went all funky
I went to the zoo, zoo
Zoo, zoo, zoo . . .

I went to the animal zoo
I wanted to go with you
I saw a girl tiger
My mum sat beside her
I went to the zoo, zoo
Zoo, zoo, zoo . . .

I went to the animal zoo
I wanted to go with you
I saw a dumb lion
My dad is called Ryan
I went to the zoo, zoo
Zoo, zoo, zoo . . .

I went to the animal zoo
I wanted to go with you
I saw a bald gorilla
I thought it was my pillow
I went to the zoo, zoo
Zoo, zoo, zoo . . .

Annie Stoneman (7)
Benhurst Primary School, Hornchurch

Eagles And Me

I just love to watch eagles
Flying gracefully in the sky
When the show has finished
I think *my, my!*
Eagles and me!

I just love to swim with dolphins
And hear their high-pitched call,
When the show has finished,
I don't want to go back to school!
Dolphins and me!

I just love to see wallabies
Jump-jumping around,
When the show has finished,
My heart starts to pound
Wallabies and me!

You see I shout, 'Wa-hoo,'
And I shout, 'We-hee,'
There's just nothing better than . . .
Hmmm . . .
Maybe . . .
Yes . . .
You guessed it!
Animals and me!

Molly Bryan (8)
Benhurst Primary School, Hornchurch

My Football Match

Thierry Henry on the ball
While I was screaming down the line,
I was shouting, 'Pass, pass,'
He passed the ball to me.

I crossed the ball to (I think)
Reyes, he hit with his left foot,
It was a screamer,
I saw the ball in the net.

I sprinted back to the halfway line
Where Reyes was celebrating,
He celebrated with me especially
We're going to win this I thought in my head.

Arsenal were still alive,
In the FA Cup final,
We wanted to get the *silverware*
In the Arsenal cabinet.

Harry Stoneman (9)
Benhurst Primary School, Hornchurch

Deep In The Jungle

Deep in the jungle
There are a lot of weird things
It is dark and scary
There are parrots but you can only see their wings.

Parrots aren't the only animals
There are gorillas and snakes
Lions, tigers, but not grizzly bears
I can't stay in this spot, the sun bakes.

There are termites in their holes
That is gross
That's a tiger
I better not get too close.

Frankie Phillips (8)
Benhurst Primary School, Hornchurch

Me The Viking Warrior

I am a Viking warrior!
Everyone calls me . . . The Soldier of Devastation
I am wearing rough animal fur,
I am rich,
So everyone addresses me as Sir.

I am laughing,
I am proud,
I am charging towards the Saxon King,
I was born to fight and not to sing.

I will tear, I will kill
I have an army but they don't care that I charge about,
Of my own freewill.

I am brave
I am proud
I am cruel,
    Because I'm a Viking warrior.

Jessie Butler (7)
Benhurst Primary School, Hornchurch

Arsenal FC

Arsenal are the best
Better than the rest,
They play so fine,
They're gonna shine.

Arsenal have won the FA Cup,
It is better than a Man U pup,
Arsenal beat Man U,
Even with their stinky shoes.

Arsenal are The Gunners,
They are faster than runners,
Arsenal use the ball,
More busier than a shopping mall.

Victor Awoniyi (9)
Benhurst Primary School, Hornchurch

The Jungle

Deep in the jungle
A tiger lay
A hippo yawns
Far away.

I saw a parrot
I might see a bee
I might see a monkey
Or a chimpanzee.

I might see an elephant
I might even see a donkey
I might see a lion
Or a monkey!

I've got my mum
I've got my dad
They are so scared
Even more than a little lad!

I hear some rustling
In a bush
It might be a lion
With ice cream round his mush!

Danielle Khick (8)
Benhurst Primary School, Hornchurch

Arsenal FC

A rsenal, Arsenal, aggravating Arsenal
R umbling Arsenal won the FA Cup!
S ensational Henry and nail-biting Bergkamp
   Complete Arsenal's 4-4-2
E ating Campbell and Ashley Cole are the team's
   Best defenders
N ever doubtful Arsenal, always win everything!
A ll teams are no better than almighty Arsenal!
L osing and losing is certainly not an option for . . .
   Almighty Arsenal!

Ajibola Lawal (9)
Benhurst Primary School, Hornchurch

Henry VIII And His Six Wives

Henry VIII had six wives,
In the end, he didn't care for their lives.

There was Catherine of Aragon and Anne Boleyn,
Both of them were nice and thin.

Henry reigned for 38 years,
All his marriages ended up in tears.

Jane Seymour surprisingly gave Henry a son,
All the other wives failed to give him one.

Henry thought Anne of Cleves was ugly,
When he divorced her, he smiled to himself smugly.

Catherine Howard was wife number five,
Her head, was cut off, she did not survive.

Katherine Parr outlived Henry,
He still lived, in her memory.

Henry VIII owned sharp spears
All the Catholics gave him sneers.

I like learning about the Tudors though,
Learning the facts that happened many years ago.

Katie Hunt (8)
Benhurst Primary School, Hornchurch

My Pet

I have a dog called Rosco
We like to have fun and play
We go for a walk all the time
Then we come back
And stay at home there all the time
The next day we have breakfast together
Then we go for another walk together
We get indoors and she goes to sleep for an hour
And then we go for another walk.

Gabrielle Woodward (8)
Benhurst Primary School, Hornchurch

Tudor Queens

Queens are very proud,
In their great castles,
Queens are very proud,
Of their beautiful clothes.

Tudor queens will live,
With their bribing goldness,
Tudor queens will live,
With their royal kings.

Tudor, Tudor, Tudor queens,
Tudor, Tudor, Tudor queens,
Tudor, Tudor, Tudor queens
It's Tudor, Tudor queens.

Queens will drink their red wine,
While putting on a dress,
Queens will drink their red wine,
While laying out the table.

Tudor queens will listen to music,
With a partner to dance with,
Tudor queens will listen to music,
As well as reading a book.

Tudor, Tudor, Tudor queens,
Tudor, Tudor, Tudor queens,
Tudor, Tudor, Tudor queens,
It's Tudor, Tudor queens.

Louisa Beckwith (9)
Benhurst Primary School, Hornchurch

Henry VIII

I am Henry, King of England,
I wear my sparkling jewels,
I can't wait to show them off,
At this evening ball.

I like to fight,
I like to win,
I like to eat,
That is my favourite thing.

I like to wear my crown,
It makes me look royal,
I like to wear my crown,
Because it makes me king!

Hannah Barker (9)
Benhurst Primary School, Hornchurch

Air Raid

Walking up the threadbare stair
Sick of make-do and mend
I hear a buzzing noise and look outside
There's light in the foggy black sky
I wonder why and how I'm here
A pain comes in my head
There's an ocean of glass on the floor
The result of a German bomber.

Nathaniel Newman (11)
Blenheim Park Community Primary School, Fakenham

Skipping In The Garden

Skipping in the garden like teddy bear
One, two, three then jump up in the air

Jumping in the garden without any care
Un, deux, trios, hop up in the air.

Hopping in the garden showing I'm not scared
One, two, three then hop up in the air.

Abbie Charlton (11)
Blenheim Park Community Primary School, Fakenham

My Kind Of School

My kind of school is . . .
An underwater school
There are a lot of underwater animals
Like clownfish, rays, seahorses and marine turtles
After school I play with the dolphin
We swim
Swim
Swim.

Emma Weller (11)
Blenheim Park Community Primary School, Fakenham

Playground Sounds

The playground's empty.

The swing squeaking silently
With the wind
Pollen flying through the air
While leaves rustle

Suddenly children are there!

Jacob Holland (10)
Blenheim Park Community Primary School, Fakenham

Rainy Day

Getting my big, yellow, shiny wellington boots on,
My massive rainproof jacket,
Reaching out for the enormous door handle,
Jumping in the first puddle I see,
This is my best day ever!

Bryony Newstead (11)
Blenheim Park Community Primary School, Fakenham

Guess Who?

Slow walker
Fast trotter
Carrot muncher
Apple cruncher
Clever jumper
Gymkhana lover
What am I?
A pony.

Alysha Childs (11)
Blenheim Park Community Primary School, Fakenham

The Moon Haiku

Giant glowing ball
Frozen crystal in the sky
Is it made from cheese?

Hannah Hewitt (10)
Blenheim Park Community Primary School, Fakenham

Playing With My Friends

*P*laying with my friends
Sun*L*ight shines in my eyes
Enjoying *A*lphabet games with the infants
They are *Y*elling far away
    *G*rowling and
    *R*oaring
    *O*ver the hills
    *U*p and away I go when the bell rings
    *N*ow our teacher says go home please
The *D*ay is done.

Rosie Hewitt (11)
Blenheim Park Community Primary School, Fakenham

Rabbit

High jumper
Ground digger
Home maker
Lettuce crumbler
Carrot nibbler
Cucumber eater
Rapid runner
Great thumper
I'm a rabbit lover.

Jake Battrick (11)
Blenheim Park Community Primary School, Fakenham

Things You Might Find Under Jake Johnny's Bed

An army of bloodsucking fleas,
The rotten sap from ancient oak trees,
A puddle of earwax gathering in a plate,
Smelly pieces of rust from the garden gate,
A leaking bottle of fat frozen overnight,
The blood of a child from when he had a fight,
Dozens of crumbs from a mouldy cheesecake,
Rotten chocolate milkshake trickling to form a small lake,
An old dead cat half-eaten by bugs,
Evil looking maggots squirming around his rugs,
Embers from the fire that he burnt his homework in,
Entrails of a squashed up rat he found in the bin,
Grease from a steak left to feed the flies,
A flattened loaf of bread chucked because it wouldn't rise,
A group of giant toenails encrusted with dirt,
A huge patch of nettles guaranteed to hurt,
A large dead bird killed by the stench,
His magnificent clarinet mangled with a wrench,
A hate letter from the principal screwed up in a ball,
A plate of his mum's carrots also known as gruel,
A ball of vomit splattered on the floor,
A small piece of chewing gum he found on the door,
The bones of a shameful girl, who tried to be his friend,
An enormous bottle of spit he made to drive his sister round the bend,
Pages of dictionaries ripped out and left to rot,
A dirty nappy from when he was a baby and slept in a cot.

Liam Hall (10)
Chigwell Primary School, Chigwell

A Soldier's Bad Night

I am glad that our leader won
Too bad for me, I am in a hospital
No nice medicine,
All the horrid medicines poisoning my skin,
Yes you guessed, I'm a damaged soldier of Henry's team,
A bow was on the floor,
With a soldier dripping with blood
Every split second the floor is covered with a new puddle of blood.
I was shot with an arrow and it hurt my shoulder.
I'm now happy and joyful, I am serving my king.
He is tall and handsome,
Charming and stylish,
He wears fine clothes,
Brooches, robes and a crown full of jewels!

Ibrahim Inayat (8)
Cleveland Junior School, Ilford

Anne Boleyn That's Me

A nne Boleyn, that's me
N eeded a son to make Henry thrilled
N ever got a son, I had a daughter
E lizabeth was her name

B eautiful she was
O h I wish I had a son
L ovely as a rose is Elizabeth though
E very day she grows so beautiful
Y esterday I was so happy to have a daughter
N ever was my life so wonderful
    Now that's all about me.

Neera Senthivel (8)
Cleveland Junior School, Ilford

Grumpy Henry VIII

My name is Henry VIII
I'm big and fat,
My friends don't talk to me,
I'm so lonely,
Since I got married,
I'm big, fat and grumpy,
I write music and dance,
I dance like the flames from the blinding sun,
Dearly I wish I was young
Just like ten years ago,
I'm not the man I was,
Grumpiness coming to me,
In the dark nights,
Oh! I wish I was young,
Like I was before.

Tobi Akinola (7)
Cleveland Junior School, Ilford

The Day I Saw My Leader Die

Oh when I saw Richard die
It was the day I'd never forget
All the dead bodies lying on the floor
It was an awful day
I saw Richard get pulled off his horse
And he got an arrow in his head too
Before he was pulled off his horse
I ran as fast as I could
The next day Richard was buried
I hope he is happy with God.

Humza Mehmood (7)
Cleveland Junior School, Ilford

The Happiest Day Of My Life

I am the third wife
I decided to marry Henry.
He was so handsome.
He said that I was a beautiful woman.
I am very rich now.
I am the queen of the world.
I gave him a boy, Edward.
What a happy day that was for me!

Mohamed Abdulkarim (8)
Cleveland Junior School, Ilford

When I Was Young

When I was young, I had red hair.
I liked writing songs.
My life was so perfect.
I liked my recorder.
I played tennis all day.
I liked to show off in front of everyone.
When I became old, my life was no longer good.
I never stood.
My hair became grey and old.

Aaron Dha (8)
Cleveland Junior School, Ilford

Oh Poor Me

Oh poor me, how sad it is to leave Henry.
He liked me the best but now I have died.
How sad he must be without me.
I was the only one who gave him a son who lived.
I died a few days after I gave birth.
Oh poor me, how sad it is to leave Henry!

Zainab Maqbool (8)
Cleveland Junior School, Ilford

Sad Anne That's Me!

This is part of my life when I am in England.
I cannot speak to Henry and
He cannot speak to me.
He married me,
But now I am divorced.
Why did Holbein paint
Me so beautiful?
Henry didn't know I was not very beautiful.
I am the ugliest lady.
What can I do now?

Ikra Ali (8)
Cleveland Junior School, Ilford

Oh I'm Rich!

Oh I'm rich,
Richer than anyone.
I can spend on anything I want.
I can make my feasts anywhere I like,
I can eat as much as I like,
I love being rich, rich, rich.
I can live as I like!
I can marry as much as I want
I'm rich, rich, rich!

Vinit Vikuntam (8)
Cleveland Junior School, Ilford

On Bosworth Field

I felt my blood pumping through my veins
I heard the drums beating and I saw axes swinging
And swords clashing.
I smelt blood on the grass and saw people lying dead.
I saw heads rolling
And heard horses neighing.

Emran Ali (7)
Cleveland Junior School, Ilford

Oh I Wish I Was Young Again

Oh when I was young,
Everything was sweet,
I was handsome,
And everyone knelt at my feet,
I had so much power, nothing could stop me,
But now I'm old everything is different,
Oh my feet are swollen and bandaged,
I can hardly walk,
Oh I wish I was young again, tall and handsome,
Oh when I was young I used to run all day,
But what happened?
Now I'm old and ugly,
Oh I wish I was young again!

Sahra Mohamed (8)
Cleveland Junior School, Ilford

The Bad Night

It's me, yes Anne Boleyn.
Waiting for my death.
Crying out loud, I wish I had a boy.
They had said bad things about me
That weren't even true.
I just wanted to have one chance, just one more please.
Once Henry loved me but then I fell out of favour.
What happened! He loved me so much but then he fell out of love.
Please just one more chance!
I will try to be brave tomorrow.

Leila Jassal (8)
Cleveland Junior School, Ilford

When I Was Young

When I was young I was very handsome.
Happy and cheerful with laughter.
My hair was red like flames.
My life was great and my face was an oval shape.
I liked playing tennis all day.
My favourite instrument was the recorder.
I liked writing many great songs.
I liked dancing and singing.
My favourite thing was riding a horse.
I hunted for deer.
But now I'm old and fat.
I'm very grumpy as well
I wish I was young again.

Ankit Patel (8)
Cleveland Junior School, Ilford

My Affectionate Wife

My affectionate wife,
She was just right for me,
I loved her more than others,
She was so glamorous.
But soon one day,
She had a baby son,
I was so delighted,
She was thrilled.
But the sadness was that the next day she died
I was despondent, heartbroken!
But later I asked if I could be buried next to her.

Mithilaa Senthivel (8)
Cleveland Junior School, Ilford

Henry VII On Bosworth Field

I was standing on Bosworth Field,
The wind was blowing my hair,
The drums were banging,
When I heard the last drum, I knew I had to fight
So I took my sword and killed people.
I saw dark red blood on the floor,
Heads rolling round and round,
Swords clashing, swinging axes.
I wanted to run away, but I had to fight for my family
The Red Lancasters,
So I killed the Yorks.
Then I saw a gold thing on the floor,
I picked it up,
I knew it was the crown of Richard III.
So I put it over my head,
At last I was king, and I was proud
When I saw Richard III lying down, dead
And I was so proud when people obeyed me.

Evandra Paulo (8)
Cleveland Junior School, Ilford

All About Henry VIII

I am really royal
I am the best king of all
So what if I'm not the man I used to be
I am proud! I am the king!
I loved my wives but they asked for it
Now I will never love them again
'Ha ha,' You know I am right
but now I've thought all about the past,
I was young, I wish I had set things right before.

Iqra Masood (8)
Cleveland Junior School, Ilford

The Bosworth Field

It was a marvellous day at Bosworth Field.
The battle lasted a day and night.
There were people laying dead on the ground,
Blood soaked on the grass.
Swords clanging with other swords.
Horses frightened, rearing in alarm.
King Richard pulled off the horse,
Calling for a force.
Someone fired an arrow and King Richard lay dead.
I saw something in the hedge,
It was King Richard's crown.
At last, now I am King Henry VII.

Uniza Zia (8)
Cleveland Junior School, Ilford

Sunny And Bouncer

Sunny was a Labrador and he was my dog,
Bouncer is a Labrador and he is my dog now.

Sunny used to bark when someone knocked on the door,
But Bouncer just sits there wagging his tail more and more.

Sunny used to growl if you went for a cuddle,
Bouncer loves it, he'll snuggle and snuggle.

Sunny used to walk all alone,
Bouncer doesn't like to walk on his own.

Sunny likes spaghetti in his bowl,
Bouncer buries his tea in a hole

In my heart Sunny will always be,
But Bouncer will always be with me.

Gemma Reed (11)
Doggetts CP School, Rochford

Poppy Day Red

People heard the explosions above them
Children sat scared in the darkness,
Clinging to their only relatives,
Wishing war would end.
Soldiers risked their lives.
Most died to save Britain,
And now we remember
Them on Poppy Day red.
The people who lost their lives.
The children left homeless,
No parents to look up to
And today we remember the soldiers who saved lives,
Risking their own.
Remember Poppy Day red.

Bethany Ellaway (10)
Doggetts CP School, Rochford

Friendship

Me and my friend
Had done our homework for school
When we broke up
To not be friends again.
But we would make up
When it was Friday the 27th May 2005.
When we made up I bought flowers.
They were lovely and furry too
And so were the daisies and roses.
And the buttercup flowers were yellow.
Imagine if you broke up
You would be upset.

Becky Roper (8)
Doggetts CP School, Rochford

Tiger, Tiger
(Inspired by 'The Tiger' by William Blake)

Tiger, tiger, burning light
In the forest of the night
Coat of flame
In lightning or rain.

Tiger, tiger, moving slow
Through the jungle eyes that glow,
Creeping through the undergrowth,
Didn't even disturb the sloth.

Tiger, tiger, danger near
In the forest smell the fear
Crouching ready to attack
Leaping on the deer's back.

Tiger, tiger, sleeping tight,
In the dead of the night
Burning, burning, burning bright,
Don't even turn out your light.

Jessica Lambert (11)
Doggetts CP School, Rochford

My Little Puppy

My little brown and white puppy
He likes to play all day
He runs around the house all day
He likes to eat all his food
He is very sweet indeed
He has very small ears
He stays with me all day.

My little brown and white puppy.

Olivia Spearman (8)
Doggetts CP School, Rochford

The Boats

I went to see the boats,
They were green, yellow, blue and brown.
They were all tied up with ropes
A long way out of town.

They were shining in the sun,
The diamonds hanging on a line
Bobbing up and down
Having fun.

I walked onto the sand
I took my shoes off
By now I was very hot
And I fell down with a plop!

Emily Davis (9)
Doggetts CP School, Rochford

All About Wind

Wind can be rough as the sea.
Wind can be smooth or calm.
Sometimes it can be fast like a racing car.
Or slow as a tortoise.
Sometimes it is *big and mighty.*
Other times it is small.
Wind can be as cold as ice,
Or can be warm or cool.
But I will share you in a little secret.
I get a bit fed up with wind,
But there is some fun in wind,
And that is flying kites.

Abby Hare (7)
Doggetts CP School, Rochford

Puppy

Loud drinker
Ankle biter
Tail wagger
Playful fighter
Noise maker
Postman chaser
Dog racer
Quick runner
Floor messer
Bin sniffer
Bottom licker
Lap snuggler.

Rebecca Ramsey (10)
Doggetts CP School, Rochford

Football

The game that I've been waiting for
The game has finally come
Here I am at the game so nervous.
Need to remember no fouls, no sliding, but passing,
To get the ball up there.
When I'm up there with the ball
Tackling them all.
Shooting and scoring with my skills.
Damn I just got fouled.
A penalty now.
I'm injured
But I score my winning goal!

Callum Soper (10)
Doggetts CP School, Rochford

Manchester United

As the blast of the crowd in your ears ring,
That means Man U are gonna win,
The opposing team falls in defeat,
Only their keeper has a clean sheet,
3 points achieved, soon a cup,
Next year we are sure to go back up,
Soon we arrive for our final game,
It's our rival Arsenal again,
So this game will be a snatch,
Will Man U win this match?
As red opposed black,
Who will carry the Cup back?
The whistle blew the game's begun,
This match ain't just for fun,
The teams both have good offence,
But who will break through each other's defence?
Finally Man U score,
But the ref disallows this as his sweat began to pour,
The game ended, score nil-nil,
It's penalties, someone must score until,
The end comes quick, Man U is in defeat,
But they smile as each team meet.

Kris Neave-Houghting (11)
Doggetts CP School, Rochford

My Dog

M y dog Trigger is so cute when his eyes glow
Y ou may be scared when you see him at first
But you'll get to know him soon enough.

D ogs are great to keep you company
O h so very cuddly, it's
G reat to have a dog.

Jade Lewin (10)
Doggetts CP School, Rochford

Cars, Mars and Stars

If you have a car
You might just go too far
Away from all the stars
While you're drinking out a jar
You might land on Mars
Away from all the stars
Or you could go to the petrol station.
Instead!

Louis Cash (10)
Doggetts CP School, Rochford

Happiness

Happiness is loads of bright colours like a rainbow.

Happiness sounds like laughter, joy and much more than that.

It feels like – well you tell me what your happiness feels like.

Peter Currell (8)
Doggetts CP School, Rochford

Sqwiffy

My cat Sqwiffy sleeps in boxes.
My cat Sqwiffy gets stuck in holes
My cat Sqwiffy fell from the garden shed
My cat Sqwiffy steals the washing
She would never hurt a fly or hiss when she's angry
All she ever does is sleep in boxes on the shed
Fall onto the washing
And land in holes.

Dean Eagle (11)
Doggetts CP School, Rochford

Insects

Some insects are slimy,
Some insects are tiny,
Some insects do look nice,
And some insects look ugly.

Insects are tiny,
Insects are slimy,
Insects look nice,
And insects look ugly.

Insects are long,
Insects are short,
Insects can chop in half,
And it doesn't hurt them at all.

Some insects are spotty,
Some insects are plain,
Some insects are naughty,
And some insects insane.

Some insects I like,
And some insects I don't,
But some are quite pretty,
Like a lovely butterfly.

Insects don't like humans,
Cos they're very tall,
Some humans don't like insects,
Because they're very cruel.

Some insects are fluffy,
Some insects are not,
And some insects are really strange,
And some insects wear socks
And I like insects
Very, very, very much!

Megan Loker (8)
Doggetts CP School, Rochford

Child Of The Darkness

When the night draws in
And the withering souls find the strength to crawl home,
To worry for another day
To pray for the strength to carry on.

The child of the darkness
Begins his nightly prowl.
The wind blows through him like a knife,
To the bone.
The darkness shields him from the life he left at home.
His steps are like thundering grey waves.
Against a huge sea wall.
His mind thinks of nothing
Except the freedom he may one day hold.
Alone he walks.
The shadows, his friends,
The darkness soothes him
And he is not so alone.

He is one of the night's children
A captured soul,
Of the war that exists.
Between night and day,
Light and darkness,
So close is the dawn,
The silver line on the horizon,
The break in the sky,
When a new day is born.

And once again he fades away,
Back to the war zone.

Lily Humpage (11)
Doggetts CP School, Rochford

That's The End Of The Rainbow

R is for red as bright as roses
O is for orange so bright it hurts my eyes
Y is for yellow, shiny like the sun
G is green, the colour of fresh grass
B is for blue, the colour of the sea where the dolphins swim
I is for indigo the colour of the night
V is violet the colour of violets swaying in the wind
                        That's the end of the rainbow poem.

Iona Walkling (9)
Doggetts CP School, Rochford

Madness And Happiness

Madness is dark red like a fuming volcano about to explode.
It sounds like a screaming maniac and a stampede coming for you.
It feels like an earthquake eating in your mind.
Happiness is a pale blue like the sea
Flowing with the wind.
It sounds like the wolves howling and the trees whooshing.
It feels like you have been hypnotised
By flowers and angels.

Chloe Newcombe (9)
Doggetts CP School, Rochford

Jogging In The Park

        I went into the park,
        I heard a dog bark.
        I was going to jog,
        And tripped over a dog.

Glen Atkin (10)
Dycorts Special School, Romford

The Postbox

A postbox looks like a man with a hat
That swallowed up my letter to Nan.
It could be a robot who spat it out
In the letter box belonging to Nan.
It looks like a policeman who's going
'Halt!'
To the man in a post office van.
If the postbox was big I'd get in it,
Wrapped up like a parcel to Nan.
I'd travel all day, I'd travel all night
And get there next day with the postman.

Harry Thomas (10)
Dycorts Special School, Romford

I Can't Wait

I will go to Florida on a jet,
I want it hot and sunny
I don't want it rainy and wet!

Joe Fordham (10)
Dycorts Special School, Romford

The Wedding

Next week my mum is to marry
My dad who is tall, handsome and great.
My mum has asked me to carry the ring,
I hope I'm not terribly late.
My brother must welcome the guests
My sister will hold hands with my mum.
We'll be dressed in our special best,
And we're all going to have such fun!

Billy Isham (10)
Dycorts Special School, Romford

Mamma You're A Real Pain

Mamma are you still in bed,
With a temperature and an itchy head?

Are you having a lovely bath,
Washing and scrubbing and having a laugh?

Mamma I know you want to look good,
But shopping and spending isn't the way you should.

You never stop staying in bed,
And Dadda pays your bills instead.

You're spending money like it's going out of fashion,
And you're buying clothes with a lot of passion.

Everyone laughs and looks and stares,
While you just walk along without any cares.

Mamma sit down, we need to talk,
We could stay here or go for a walk.

There's something we need to chat about,
Please Mamma, do not shout.

It's just that all our money's gone,
So now we'll have to call upon . . .

Georgina Power (11)
East Winch CE (VA) Primary School, King's Lynn

Strawberries

Strawberry pie, lemon and lime
Give me them, they're all mine
Yummy thick cream and sugar on top
Is more bright red strawberries. I can't stop!
I've eaten too much, I think I'm fat
I think I will explode, well fancy that!
Scrumptious strawberries in my tummy,
I like them, they're so *yummy!*

Chelsea Palmer (10)
East Winch CE (VA) Primary School, King's Lynn

All About Witches

Witches, britches
Boils and itches
Potions bubbling
Like lava.

Witches, bats
Curdled with
Rats and you'll
Never see them again.

Witches' skin
Green and thin
Rough with a
Greasy surface.

Witches' eyes look
Like lies
You'll never trust
Her again.

Witches, britches
Boils and itches
Potions bubbling,
Like lava.

Haley Knowles (12)
East Winch CE (VA) Primary School, King's Lynn

Guinea Pigs

Guinea pigs are fluffy
They run across so speedily
Very tiny, like a rat with no tail
When you let them out they are so jumpy
Very sharp claws like a bald eagle
They are neat by pooing in corners!

Matthew Atkin (10)
East Winch CE (VA) Primary School, King's Lynn

A Winter Night

The freezing night strolling down the street
The bitter cold snow was getting to my once warm feet
Every time I turned around the breeze was making whooshing sounds.
Walking past pretty shop windows in the street
Happiness and laughter sinking to my feet.

Amy Cross (7)
East Winch CE (VA) Primary School, King's Lynn

Need For Speed

Need for speed
I am about to take the lead.
Drafting behind and tuned at my top speed.
Racing down a wide street,
With my music at a fast beat.
It is so loud it is making me bob up
And down in my sparco seat!
Just about to push the button that will
Hopefully accelerate me straight into the lead.
The finish is in my sight,
The glory is going to be mine tonight.
My Nissan Skyline just gave them all a
Horrible fright.

Alex Parkinson (11)
East Winch CE (VA) Primary School, King's Lynn

My Pirate Friend

Hairy like a mad wolf.
Crazy like a fast talking parrot.
Dirty like a pig in a mud puddle.
Scary like a roaring lion.
Scruffy like a porcupine.
Angry like a gorilla
Is my pirate friend.

Thomas Bailey (8)
East Winch CE (VA) Primary School, King's Lynn

Cool Cat

Jet-black
Yellow eyes like car lights
Claws like knives
Tail like a pencil
Curled like a ball.

Perry Large (11)
East Winch CE (VA) Primary School, King's Lynn

Birthdays

Birthdays are the best time of year
Sparkling presents everywhere
I'm so excited
And delighted
I can't wait until it gets here!

What presents will I get?
A fast car or a toy jet
A pram or a huge doll's house
Or a wind up toy mouse
Or even my own pet?

Laura Wilson (9)
East Winch CE (VA) Primary School, King's Lynn

The Revolting Rabbit

At the bottom of the garden
There is a hutch
In the hutch there is a white rabbit
The white rabbit has big teeth
The white rabbit has big teeth and a loud roar . . .
The white rabbit has big teeth, a loud roar and stamping feet.
The white rabbit has big teeth, a loud roar, stamping feet
                                        and big floppy ears.
The white rabbit eats bees and climbs trees!

Emily Gooding (8)
East Winch CE (VA) Primary School, King's Lynn

Dolphin

How I long to be a dolphin,
Swimming in the sea,
Does anyone else want to be free?

Catching fish and leaping high,
Jumping till I reach the sky,
How wonderful and fun,
Anybody, anyone?

Playing with my family,
Swimming along in the sea.

I'd be the smartest dolphin there ever was,
Don't ask why, just because!

So just remember dolphins are great,
Never, ever, ever hate.

Oh how I long to be a dolphin . . .

Ellie-Jo Hodgson (11)
Eversley Primary School, Basildon

The Sea

The deep, blue, sapphire sea twinkles in the moonlight
The aquatic undulation of waves ripples and rolls.
White horses gallop from sea to shore beautifully.
Dolphins break the sea with their awesome beauty.
Fish swim swift on the sea's sandy bottom leaving clouds of dust.
The ocean is so beautiful.
Dolphins dive in the shimmering sights of the shadow.
The sea gives birth to wavelets every moment.
The moonlight twinkles with shadows on the sea's surface.
The
Ocean
Is
So
Beautiful.

Lacey Brooks (11)
Eversley Primary School, Basildon

A Sea Haiku

The sea is sodden
The sea is tempestuous
Where yachts travel slow.

Benjamin Robinson (10)
Eversley Primary School, Basildon

The Sea Cinquain

The sea
It calls for me.
With glorious tall waves
Stalking, waiting, daring me to -
Jump in.

Holly Philpot (11)
Eversley Primary School, Basildon

One Little Fishy

On the bottom of the deep sea blue
Lived the fishy swimming through.
In the coral under the sea,
Lies the treasure waiting for me.

But when one fishy swam into the black
He was never ever to come back
He didn't know that it was oil
All he could do was coil, coil, coil.

He put his head in his scales
And then he got swallowed by some whale,
In the whale's tummy he thought he was safe,
Hoping that he could escape.

In the tummy
All he wanted was his mummy
And in the end he would suffocate
And that swim was a big, big mistake!

Jack Dickinson (11)
Eversley Primary School, Basildon

Mixed Up Ocean

You Sea, you're a foul, boisterous, animal
But a tranquil place to chill,
A hazardous congested ocean,
Oh Sea, what mixed feelings I feel!

You have an odourous, almighty home,
But a gleaming, invisible coat.
The white horses are your security guards,
And the sand is your coastline moat.

Why are you open to the public Sea?
Just think of all the people you've killed . . .
They were just out for a family day,
You should be caught and sealed.

You Sea, you're a foul, boisterous, animal
But a tranquil place to chill,
A hazardous, congested ocean,
Oh Sea, what mixed feelings I feel!

Charlotte Nicholls (10)
Eversley Primary School, Basildon

The Seaside

The sea clashes with the cliffs
Like two wrestlers in a ring.
The wind dives and slices into the sea
Making the sea angry and making a fountain of spray.
The waves charge up the beach like cars on a road,
Wiping clean the sand like a cloth on a whiteboard.
The sea has no friends,
People come and play in him, but that makes him angry
So he tries to swallow them using terrifying waves
Like teeth until he wins.

Jake Batten (11)
Eversley Primary School, Basildon

World War II In Britain

W here the young children fled
O nto a safe place
R unning low on food, not overfed
L ots of Germans being a disgrace
D eaths were caused every day.

W ith everyone so scared
A nyone ran to the underground railway
R uins were tried to be repaired.

2 nd worst terrible war in the whole world

I n the seas nothing was safe
N ot even a submarine

B loodstained bullets everywhere
R otten Germans tried to win
I n every way
T oo many Britains to let them win
A country here to defeat
I n everyway
N orth, south, east and west
   Put them together we beat the rest.

Samantha Reeve (11)
Harleston CE (VA) Primary School

World War II

World War II was very frightening
Bombs flew through the air like lightning,
Hitler was very mad,
When Germany fought bad,
England won, it was exciting.

Amy Leeder (10)
Harleston CE (VA) Primary School

The Olympics

T he Olympics is held every four years
H ere is where enjoyment makes tears
E very four years lots of athletes compete.

O n every occasion under the heat
L ives are sometimes risked
Y our heart jumps when a move is missed
M oments of madness as people fight
P ermanently using all of their might
I nto the starting blocks athletes go
C heering them on as they start on their toe.

G ymnasts do all of their tricks
A ll in applause as they do their kicks
M edals are awarded at the end of the games
E ven losers achieved their aims
S miles on the winners' faces.

Rhian Earrye (11)
Harleston CE (VA) Primary School

World War II

W is for world at war
O is for ordinary people being killed for no reason
R is for ruined buildings everywhere
L is for lives destroyed by the war
D is for damage done to houses.

W is for war, cruel and sad
A is for air raids when the bombs are dropped
R is for running to the shelters.

T is for trenches where the soldiers sleep
W is for women doing all the jobs
O is for obedient soldiers doing what they're told.

Stephanie Knox (11)
Harleston CE (VA) Primary School

Hitler

Peace ender
Money maker
Life taker
Ground shaker
People beater.
Hitler.

Sinead Carey (11)
Harleston CE (VA) Primary School

Spitfire

S peeding through the sky
P rotectors of Britain
I n the sky shooting down the Germans
T he planes being scrambled
F iring at other planes
I dentified with letters and numbers
R adioing back to base
E ach with its own pilot.

Andrew Langham-Service (11)
Harleston CE (VA) Primary School

Rivers

R unning water splashing
I n and out of trees
V ery cold and crystal clear
E very drop from the sky
R emakes rivers once again
S plashing, splashing, *splash!*

Devon Green (10)
Harleston CE (VA) Primary School

The Computer Game

There once was a boy with a key,
Who went on holiday to sea,
He found a large cave,
So he started to save,
And then he got stung by a bee.

Then suddenly he woke up,
It was all a big mix-up,
He had dreamt of this game,
When he had a nickname,
And then in came a grown-up.

Douglas Webber (11)
Harleston CE (VA) Primary School

World War II Haiku

Hitler was insane,
Because he shot all our planes,
Now we all complain.

Jack Lovick (11)
Harleston CE (VA) Primary School

Plants And Flowers

Water wanderers
Sunlight seekers
Leafy lovers
Soil soakers
Blooming buds
Pretty petals
Plants and flowers!

Danielle Hines (11)
Harleston CE (VA) Primary School

World War II

Monday
The war began
And everyone ran.

Tuesday
They start to bomb
It went on for quite long.

Wednesday
Always carry your gas mask
And sometimes have a flask.

Thursday
Grow your own food
It has got me in a good mood.

Friday
Britain flew to bomb
Germany was long.

Saturday
Children who are evacuated
Didn't have a bed.

Sunday
People ran round and round
They lined up in the underground.

Matthew Buchan (11)
Harleston CE (VA) Primary School

WWII

Lots of bombs gliding through the air,
People knew Hitler didn't care,
Parents going insane,
Children being a pain
World War II was a nightmare.

Kyle Kenneally (11)
Harleston CE (VA) Primary School

A Lonely Bear

My brown hair is black
My button nose is lost
One of my eyes is missing
And I remain forgotten.

I've lived on this cupboard
For the past twenty years,
I'm all alone
And nobody knows I'm here.

I want to be loved
I want to be hugged
I want to be back
In the little girl's arms.

With no nose,
Black fur,
And only one eye
I will never be loved.

I will be all alone
For the rest of my days
I am dirty and smelly
And there is nobody to love me.

Vicki Scofield (11)
Harleston CE (VA) Primary School

Tsunami Poem

Children crying in the midnight sky
Waves crashing as people die
Hotels falling to the ground
When shops lose every pound
And people look for their family.

Alex Burlton (10)
Harleston CE (VA) Primary School

War

There was a man called Mr Hoor
Who wanted to go to the war,
He went off to train,
But missed the aeroplane,
And he ended up being poor.

Isabel Cockle (11)
Harleston CE (VA) Primary School

Planes

Bomb dropper
City killer
Life destroyer
People scarer
Death causer
Factory bomber
Street burner
Dog fighting
Home wrecker
Planes!

Charlie Oakes (10)
Harleston CE (VA) Primary School

Science

Science is very, very fun
You have to get everything done
You do loads, loads and loads
You go through different modes
Then everyone is on the run.

Danielle O'Connor (10)
Harleston CE (VA) Primary School

They Come Tanka

Roman ships appear
Out of mist and on to shore
Their armour shining
They win and conquer Britain
Bringing their culture to us.

Joe Collins (10)
Harleston CE (VA) Primary School

War

W ar is a horrible thing
O ften people ignored the raids
R aids had buildings down
L ondon was Hitler's main target
D ead were hundreds of thousands.

W inston Churchill held England's light
A ir raid wardens had hectic nights
R oyal Navy did their part

2 many lives were lost.

James Baker (11)
Harleston CE (VA) Primary School

World War II Limerick

All the bombs are dropping on us
So much we're getting furious
It's making us crazy
And then maybe lazy
And soon it'll make us pompous.

Bronwyn Elsden (11)
Harleston CE (VA) Primary School

Britain

B old and brave
R ough and tough
I ncredible
T he ones to trust
A live and well
I moveable object
N ot giving up.

Kane Peacock (11)
Harleston CE (VA) Primary School

Rivers

Rain dribbling from the sky
Leaving the leaves in see-through dye,
Water trickles down hills
And leaks till it fills
Darting through mountains up high.

Emma Jackson (11)
Harleston CE (VA) Primary School

A Night In The Blitz Tanka

The bombs are dropping
We are in the Anderson
Can you hear them drop?
The Nazis are invading
I may not return outside.

Rory James (11)
Harleston CE (VA) Primary School

Animals From India

Tiger
Cub cuddler
Body camouflager
Buffalo pouncer
Prey watcher
Nose twitcher
Animal catcher
Tiger!

Indian elephant
Trunk swayer
Water sprayer
Tail wagger
Feet stomper
Mouse hater
Peanut eater
Indian elephant!

Emma Earye (11)
Harleston CE (VA) Primary School

The Fortress

The bright blue water
The shining sun on the rocks
Along the orange rocks
Lies the rugged cliff.

A beautiful sight and a calm sea
A massive fortress defended by walls of rock.
You can still hear the boats
Right at the top is a beacon
And under the water there lies a hole full of darkness.
You will always remember the heat, the rock,
The sand, the water.

Luke Bellingham (10)
John Bunyan Junior School, Braintree

The Ice Mountain

The ice mountain,
The glittering mound,
How did it get there?
When was it found?
Has it been found?
Am I the first one here?
I don't know, I'll never find out.

It's a wonderful place, a beautiful place,
I've never been here before,
To the ice mountain.

It's shimmering in the sun,
It looks like it's going to melt down.
It's dripping in the heat,
It's calling to me to come to it,
To cool me down.

It's my favourite place,
To come and rest,
I'd come here again
To the ice mountain.

Steven Wheeler (11)
John Bunyan Junior School, Braintree

A Season

An opening flower is like the seed of life.
It brings us happiness and joy.
The trees are our strength, but give us air.
Life is our energy but gives us joy.
Water gives us health and our spirit.
Birds give us inner feeling and emotional feeling.
Doves give us peace and harmony.
The wind gives us life and season.
The sun brings us to one season and it is
Spring!

Caleb Wicker (8)
John Bunyan Junior School, Braintree

Cliff Spring Falls

I always wonder abut Cliff Spring Falls
Why the water goes down the walls,
Splish, splash, splish, splash,
That's what I hear when the waters crash.

I always wonder about the Cliff Spring walls
How did they get there? Why are they so tall?
When pouring the water looks white
Although the walls block my sight.

I always wonder about the Cliff Spring trees
The way they shake and wave in the breeze,
For some reason the water looks black
As it oozes, trickles and falls through the cracks.

I always wonder about Cliff Spring Falls
Why the spring seems to call
The way the water corrodes the walls,
That's why I wonder about Cliff Spring Falls.

Ryan Harris (11)
John Bunyan Junior School, Braintree

The Volcano

The hole . . . the hole . . .
Filled with fire
Starting to burn
I feel as if it's going to burn the land,
I see that the black bits are dead
I believe the red bits are alive.
I feel that I will burn!
The heat of the fire will destroy the land!
I feel as if I should follow it.
I am imagining going to this fantasy land . . .
I wonder where it leads to . . .
I believe the hole underneath the surface
It is filled with beautiful light.
I imagine the light shows something.

Kelvin Chuttur (10)
John Bunyan Junior School, Braintree

The Giant's Causeway

Cold stony eyes looking straight back at me.
Laying on wet crumbly sand.
With frothy water surrounding these amazing things,
All I can hear is the water smashing against the rocks,
Making a wonderful sound,
You can hardly believe where I am,
It's a magical place,
Who knows what is hidden beneath the incredible surface,
What made it?
How was it made?
No one knows,
And no one ever will.

Amy Spooner (11)
John Bunyan Junior School, Braintree

From Turquoise To Azure

A tiny island
Surrounded by sea
The clouds hovering above it
The clear sea
Travelling along
To the huge ocean.

If you look further
Than your eyesight can take you
You can find
That the sea has almost swallowed
The whole island.

The palm tree swaying
In the cool empty breeze
All alone
While the sea is travelling
To distant places
The waves turn from turquoise to azure.

Tyler Duchar-Clark (10)
John Bunyan Junior School, Braintree

The Hand Of Hope

The crystalline water shimmering in the perfect sunlight,
The deserted isle like a grain of sand out in the ocean
The palm tree swaying like a hand
Waving goodbye to all hope
The shades of blue venturing further
Into the depths of the deep blue sea.

Thomas Ranson (10)
John Bunyan Junior School, Braintree

Teddy

Teddy is soft, cuddly and squidgy
He is pink, blue, green, yellow and white
I tuck him under the duvet at bedtime
And when it's dark, I squeeze him tight.

Teddy is soft, cuddly and squidgy
We get together when the stars come out at night
And when I turn off my bed lamp
All I see are his eyes sparkling bright.
    Goodnight!

Beth Pasfield (9)
John Bunyan Junior School, Braintree

Nasty Weather

There'll be rain and snow
And black clouds forever
Oh no not more
Bad spells of weather!

Ben Wiseman (8)
John Bunyan Junior School, Braintree

The Blinded Sky

The blinded sky
Covered in a veil of darkness
It's a broom sweeping the heavens
Patching up all the light
Like ripped trousers sewn up
Then flashing lights light up the universe
The wolves howl and roam the wilderness
And owls awake
Suddenly a silver crescent appears
Like polished shoes it shines
Gleaming and reflecting on the waters
Who knows who lives there?
Then it goes away
Vanished it seems
Never to return until it rises again.

Colbran Tokley (11)
John Bunyan Junior School, Braintree

The Raging Waterfall

Glittery water falling down
Crystals smashing against the ground
She must be sad
As she freezes mad
Clashing against the ground
A river of jewels
Sparkling in white
The plants look dead
Shivering in their white bed
Even though they're full of life
It doesn't matter to them
As long as the water still flows.

Cornelius O'Leary (11)
John Bunyan Junior School, Braintree

Caribbean Paradise

Only room for a single palm tree
Parts of it glistening under the water.

Uninhabited by anything except for the occasional bird
White sand reflecting the burning sea.

Bright blue sky without a cloud in sight
The seabed as colourful as the nylon pool.

Palm trees moving like a Hawaiian dancer
The only land for miles around.

I can feel the scorching heat on my face
And the untouched sand between my toes.

More than half of it flooded by water
Waves approaching from every angle.

David Roberts (11)
John Bunyan Junior School, Braintree

Snap Crack And Pop

The shimmering clear crystal ice,
Cracking in my ear.
The glittering sparkle,
Beaming in my eyes.
The ice starting to melt,
Leaving the lovely popping frost.
The amazing water falling,
From the hill making me cheerful.
The icy white tree frosted over,
Gleaming in the sun.
The white ice slippy,
Platform fading away.
Me staring at the wonderful sight,
Never looking away.

Rebecca Pitcher (10)
John Bunyan Junior School, Braintree

Animals

Giraffes are tall
Ants are small
Leopards leap
Birds that cheep
They're all animals.

Rabbits hop
With ears that flop
Cats that purr
Dogs with fur
They're all animals.

The tortoise is slow
And has far to go
A sea horse that floats in the sea
I'd love to take all the animals home with me
Even the monkeys that swing in the trees.

Amber Clarey (9)
John Bunyan Junior School, Braintree

I Walked

I walked through the peaceful forest
The trees were orange and rusty.
Animals were hiding
Flowers were swaying in the breeze
I was lost and scared
The sun was shining all over me
No people came.

I became sleepy in the dark
But there was nowhere to go
No churches near me anywhere.

Danielle Read (9)
John Bunyan Junior School, Braintree

I Feel . . .

I feel calm
I feel happy
That's what I feel.
I feel peaceful
I feel graceful
That's what I feel.
I see animals dancing in the fields
I see swaying flowers
That's what I see.
I see joyful children
That's what I see.
I feel fresh air on my shoulders
I feel warm inside
That's what I feel
That's what I feel.

Jorden Stedman (8)
John Bunyan Junior School, Braintree

Rabbits

Rabbits hopping all around up high in the air
And down low on the ground.
Rabbits with long ears and rabbits with short ears.
Rabbits with bushy tails.
Rabbits with fluffy tails.
Rabbits droppings lay on the ground
In the gardens, in the parks.
Rabbits lie on cold slabs.
Hopping down into their burrows
Till dawn breaks.
The sun goes down.
Out comes the sun
Rabbits come out to play
Hopping down the streams today.

Lynsey Colbert (8)
John Bunyan Junior School, Braintree

The Country

The country is a beautiful place
A river glimmers in the sun
Children outside having fun
Sheep are eating fresh, green grass.

Hedgehogs waking in the night,
Walking around at night, some people might.
Everything's quiet in the night.

In the winter the trees are bare
No rabbits or hares
All the ducks are migrating.

Children ride bikes
And some people hike,
Lovely hills to discover
What a lovely place!

Drew Rogers (8)
John Bunyan Junior School, Braintree

Crystal Berg

The freezing ice slowly melting . . .
Dripping slowly, making a chime,
The deep, dark blue shadows,
From where the sun doesn't shine, the crystals don't
Shimmer and glisten,
The pure blue sky without a cloud in sight,
As cold as a whole world of ice.
The crystals climb to the top of the ice mountain,
Glimmering and reflecting the sun on their way.
The penguin waddles on the sheet of ice,
A land of his own to roam.

Natalie Butler (11)
John Bunyan Junior School, Braintree

Fruity

Oranges, apples, bananas, pears,
Which ones the best?
Who cares
Strawberry, mango
Which one is it?
They're both nice,
I must admit it.
Mix them together to make a drink,
That would be really nice, I think.
Drink it,
Drink it,
Drink it all up,
Drink the last bit right out of your cup.

I'esha Lewin (8)
John Bunyan Junior School, Braintree

The Blue And Yellow Beach

The sand is yellow
The sea is blue
Children are making sandcastles
Yellow and bright.

Girls and boys are swimming in the sea
The sun shines brightly
The breeze is warm
We all have ice cream.

We find all kinds of shells
I found a lovely shell,
The smell is cool,
Crabs crawl across the sand,
So come to the blue and yellow beach.

Sophie Clark (9)
John Bunyan Junior School, Braintree

Friends

Friends are for helping,
Friends get help when you are hurt,
Friends are loyal and you can trust them.

Friends help you do work,
Friends provide you with rubbers,
Friends also provide you with rulers.

Friends can assist you,
Friends help you spell correctly,
Friends help you approach your goal in school.

Ben Nichols (9)
John Bunyan Junior School, Braintree

Cloud Haiku

White clouds floating by,
Gently and softly near me,
I so like the clouds.

Sydnee Collins (8)
John Ray Junior School, Braintree

Winter

Winter is when snowdrops drop from the sky.
Winter is when it gets colder and colder.
Winter is when people get cold,
Winter is when I get cold.

Winter is when people wrap up warm,
Winter is people on snowboards,
When I go in I am bored.

Lauren Wiffen (8)
John Ray Junior School, Braintree

People

There are people all around us.
There are people everywhere.
There are people in the town and in ships.
There are lots of noises wherever people go.
People are in their garden and people are in the grocery store.
People are on planes when you fly and people are in countries
All over the world,
But the best person in the world is me.

Aaron Benfield (8)
John Ray Junior School, Braintree

Eagle Haiku

A huge bird flying
It flies like a blur of light,
It swoops to its home.

Portia Boehmer (8)
John Ray Junior School, Braintree

Roses

Roses grow day by day
Night by night.
They have red thick petals
And green bright stalks.
Some are white, and some are yellow, even pink.
Roses come in summer
When the hot sun is bright,
I wish I had a rose,
One that's red,
One yellow and even pink.
I'll put them in my favourite vase
To live forever and ever.

Molly Poulton (8)
John Ray Junior School, Braintree

Summer

Summer is the green grass swaying in the breeze.
Summer is the chocolate melting.
Summer is when the days get longer.
Summer is when the days get brighter.
Summer is when the days get hotter.
Summer is when I can go to the country
And have a picnic.
Summer is when lemonade goes flat.
Summer is the best days of my life.
Summer is when the sunbeams shine.

Charlotte Hughes (8)
John Ray Junior School, Braintree

The Shark

There is a shark in the sea and it has sharp teeth.
It is fierce and big!
    Also it is very strong.
    It doesn't sleep at night because it will die.
    And it lives in the sea.

Gabriella Mackay (8)
John Ray Junior School, Braintree

Summer

Summer is fun
Summer is when you have a water fight.
Summer is when the sun glows.
In the summer you have ice cream.
Summer is when you play with your mates
Until the sun goes down.
Summer is so much fun, it is the best season in the world.
I love the summer, do you?

Thomas Jarman (8)
John Ray Junior School, Braintree

Cloud Haiku

The white clouds flow by
As soft as silk like a quilt
Sometimes it turns grey.

Lauren Chambers (8)
John Ray Junior School, Braintree

Sad I Ams

I am . . .
The empty cola can that no one bothered to recycle
The football that no one pumped up.

I am . . .
The house that no one lives in
The flower that someone squashed.

I am . . .
The bird that someone shot
The child, unwanted.

I am . . .
      Myself.

Shannon Gates (8)
John Ray Junior School, Braintree

Trees

Trees all around
Trees that pound
Trees that sound
As quiet as an ant
Trees that rustle
With a great big muscle
I will not break a tree.

Eren Tokkan (8)
John Ray Junior School, Braintree

The Sea Horse

I saw a sea horse swimming
In the ocean.

I caught up with it
Then I started to swim with it.

Charlotte Willett (8)
John Ray Junior School, Braintree

The Old Tramp

There was a man in a big town
Who saw a tramp stealing
Money from a shop.
The old man got a van
And went to get a cop.
Policeman came and took away
The tramp with a bag of money.
The police smiled but the
Tramp said it wasn't very funny.

Sean Keeling (7)
John Ray Junior School, Braintree

My Sister Haiku

My sister is loud.
My sister is annoying.
My sister's smelly.

Charlotte Rossiter (7)
John Ray Junior School, Braintree

Walking And Talking

Today I am talking.
Next day I am walking.
Next day I was talking about walking to school.
After I was gabbing about different languages.

James Best (7)
John Ray Junior School, Braintree

The Dolphins

The wet, soft
        Dolphins

Diving down,
        Down
  Into the sea.
Swimming, swimming through the deep sea.

Rebecca Elsey (8)
John Ray Junior School, Braintree

The Bad Cat

The bad cat was so bad he
Scared dogs
So bad they hid behind logs.
And other cats ran up trees to hide
They waited and they came down with a slide.

Jordan Pannell (8)
John Ray Junior School, Braintree

My Family

My family goes everywhere
Together like tiny particles
In a solid.
Families are great because
Everyone likes me like
Monkeys like their bananas.

My family is sometimes
Annoying like a load of birds pecking at me.
Families are super because
They live all over the world
And live in weird hot and cold places
Like France and act like cheetahs
Running all over the place
Trying to catch their prey.

Families are nice because
They go to the park with you
And act like children.
Families are the best because
They let you have crazy sleepovers
That they can act really mad
Around us.
Families are brilliant because
They can spoil you with all the money
That they have got
I love my family because they are like cheeky monkeys
That love me and bananas.

Charlotte McNamara (10)
Morland Primary School, Ipswich

Holidays

Holidays make you feel relaxed
On a boat on a boiling summer's day
With the water rushing to the shore
Like white horses running towards you.

Holidays make me feel full of joy
When I go on a summer holiday
Running about on the smooth sand
Swimming around in the sparkling sea.

The sparkling sea goes onto your feet
It may be cold
As cold as ice
But it will get as hot as the sun.

Holidays make me feel happy
Laying in the hot summer sun
The cool breeze will blow on your face.

Kira Wymer (10)
Morland Primary School, Ipswich

The Never Ending School Holiday!

Holidays off school are fabulous fun,
They make me feel like I will explode like a volcano
With excitement.

Holidays off school are fabulous fun,
They're brilliant, they're fun, they're like standing in an extra fun,
Crashing and bashing waterfall.

Holidays off school are fabulous fun,
They make me feel happy and I don't know about you
But they make me feel all oogly in my tummy.

Holidays off school are fabulous fun,
They're great, they're amazing, they're like jumping in a really,
Really magical tunnel!

Rochelle Rankin (9)
Morland Primary School, Ipswich

My Holiday

When I heard that we were going to Spain
My face lit up as the lightning struck.
We were getting on the aeroplane,
In two days of resting and cooling,
We were there.

The sea was amazing
The waves were wild
I could tell this holiday was going to be great.
I thought
No school,
No homework
And no one telling me what to do.

All we did was on the beach
Because it was so gorgeous
I sunbathed the whole time
I got burnt and brown all over.

We had to leave, so we packed our stuff,
Got on the plane.
I fell asleep halfway.
When I woke up we were home again.

Jasmine Fairs (10)
Morland Primary School, Ipswich

At The Beach

The beach is a huge bowl of custard
Sitting in the world,
The sand is as yellow as a newborn chick.

Water is blue that reminds me of the sky up above,
And the sky reminds me of the water below
And that is the beach.

There are clouds as fluffy as sheep
But best of all is the sun setting
It is as if it can jump up and down in slow motion.

Leanne Goldsmith (9)
Morland Primary School, Ipswich

My Crazy Family

My mum always cleans the house like birds
Building a perfect nest.
She shouts at my brother like a rooster on top
Of a barn first thing in the morning.
She never shouts at me because I'm her sweet angel.

My dad is cool like hamsters with sunglasses
Climbing on top of the cage.
He can dance like sheep running
And when he jumps in the swimming pool
He is like a whale, splashing into the sea.
He screeches old songs like a radio playing old songs.

My brother sits on the couch all day
Like a lazy cow eating grass
He plays on the PS2 like a spider crawling.

My family eat like monkeys munching bananas.

Jennifer Mok (10)
Morland Primary School, Ipswich

My Family

There's too many people in this family,
We all like different things,
Some like playing,
Some like music,
Some like anything.

My dad likes Elvis,
My mum's a bookworm,
I'm a card collector,
My uncle's like a computer genius
My aunt's a DVD maker,
My brother is just a plain old brother.

There's too many people in my family,
We all like different things.

Adam Keevil (10)
Morland Primary School, Ipswich

My Holiday

When I'm on holiday
I enjoy it so much
I enjoy it so much
I feel like I'm a fish
Swimming in a cool fresh ocean!

When I'm on holiday
I enjoy sitting around
A big fire cooking
Marshmallows on sticks.
I feel like a monkey
Eating lots of bananas!

When I'm on holiday
There is one thing I'm scared of.
I'm scared I will get sunburn!
I'll feel as red
As a lobster!

Amena Ali (9)
Morland Primary School, Ipswich

Holidays

The sun is beaming
The clouds are gone
We go to the arcades
Explore the place
Buy what you want where you want
It's like volcano beaming with sun
It's a holiday!

The sea is warm,
The sand is soft,
The sun is hot,
The fish are swimming,
It's a holiday!

Josh McNamee (10)
Morland Primary School, Ipswich

My Holiday

The perfect way
To relax, swim and play.
No work.
No school.
We're on a
Holiday.

All my troubles are forgotten.
I've no worries in the world.
My mum is at the bar,
And I'm relaxing like
There is no tomorrow.

With a magazine in one hand,
And a glass of cool, icy lemonade in the other,
Sunbathing on the hot, soft sand,
As firm as sugar.

The sound of the waves
Jumping over the sea.
The cool, swift breeze of the night
Swimming to my nose to cool me down.

The clubs with people dancing to the beat
Tapping to the rhythm.

The perfect way to relax, swim and play
We're on a holiday.

My mum snoring like a big fat pig.
While I'm swimming in the pool.

I'm sad to say,
It's the last day.

In the sky,
Flying like a butterfly.

We're home
It's a shame
But I hated it
On that aeroplane!

Brady Todd (10)
Morland Primary School, Ipswich

On My Holiday

On my holiday
I went to Great Yarmouth
To the seaside
The sun was like lava pouring
From a volcano.

The sky stretched
Far across the clouds
Like a giant elastic band.

The sand was as yellow
As custard.
The stones were as shiny as
A hard polished floor.

The waves were
As smooth as
Melted soft cheese.

On my holiday I laid in the soft
Chocolate, making a snowman.

Curtis Saunders (9)
Morland Primary School, Ipswich

My Family

My family are like five peas in a pod.
All of us get along and we play games
With each other and we make each other laugh.

My family are like lions
We always stick up for each other
When we fight the outside world
And we stick together.

My family are like hyenas.
We always have fun and have a laugh together.

Bethany Mortimer (9)
Morland Primary School, Ipswich

Loads Of Friends

I have loads of friends because of my good looks.
My looks are like a kind person strolling down the street.
I have loads of friends because of my name.
I'm named after Grant Mitchell.
I have loads of friends because of my family,
My family is very popular around the estate.

I have loads of friends because of my stuff.
My stuff is in good condition.
I have loads of friends because of my Ferrari PS2.
My Ferrari PS2 is worth over two hundred pounds.
I have loads of friends because of my pets.
My pets are as cute as anything.

I have loads of friends because of their names.
Their names are like mine.
I have loads of friends because of the things I do.
I do things that make them laugh for hours.
I have loads of friends because of the things I say.
I say funny things to my bunch of friends.

Grant Day (9)
Morland Primary School, Ipswich

Jack's Boat

Upon my boat I float across the open sea.
We float in my boat as far as you can see.
The wind takes me far away,
I have come a long way today.
I must go back before night falls.
The tide is turning we could look like fools!

Jack Burke (8)
Newtons Primary School, Rainham

Planets!

The Earth with its core bubbling hot
And its oceans stretched wide for all to see

The moon with its lunar dust controlling the tides
Of the sea on the Earth
And its craters deep down to its core

Jupiter, its desert surface stretched all around
And its sandstorms terrorising everything in their path

Mercury with its burning temperatures in the day at 240°C
And its freezing temperatures at night at -270°C

Mars with its red surface blazing alight in the Milky Way
And shining on nearby planets

Pluto with its sapphire-blue surface shining like the sea
And its iron core as solid as rock

The sun with its burning temperatures
And its core spinning like a tornado
It shines out in the universe for all to see.

Maherban Lidher (11)
Newtons Primary School, Rainham

The Rainbow

Green as some juicy grass
Purple as sweet as a blackberry.
Pink as a pig.
Red as a sweet strawberry.
Blue as the sea.
Orange as a juicy orange.
Yellow as a lemon.

Abbie Wyatt (8)
Newtons Primary School, Rainham

I Want A Pet

I want a pet,
I want one now,
But I don't know what to have.

A dog, a cat,
A bird or mouse,
Or maybe just a fish.

Sometimes it is like a fluffy ball,
It climbs and it is lazy.

It wags its tail
All day long
And greets me with a kiss.

It scutters across
Wooden floors,
It nibbles and scratches,
No matter what type it is.

Standing on its perch
All multicoloured,
Chewing up his toys
Making a load of noise.

In the water
Blowing bubbles,
Swimming to and from.

What one should I have.
Do you know?

Jessica Palmer (11)
Newtons Primary School, Rainham

Flower Poem

There once was a flower
Who sat on a tower
In the sky so blue
Looking pretty just for you.

Shanyce Duffy (8)
Newtons Primary School, Rainham

What Is White?

White are the clouds
Up in the sky
Floating so gently
Oh so high.

White is a ghost
When you get a fright
When you're alone
In the middle of the night.

White is the snow
Falling through the air
Children playing happily
They have no care.

White is the wool
From a baby sheep
White is the snow
Laying in a heap.

White is innocence
Like pages in a book
Never been written on
Never had a look.

Jessie Kivuitu (9)
Newtons Primary School, Rainham

The Girl Called Jill Who Took A Pill

There was a young girl called Jill
Who loved to take a pill
She got so drunk
She became a punk
And now she's always ill.

Jordan Nastri (10)
Newtons Primary School, Rainham

The Very Silly Frog

There once was a man called Frog
He loved to sit on the bog
He fell down the hole
And got a big mole
And now he sleeps in the fog.

Maria Rolfe (10)
Newtons Primary School, Rainham

Going Bonkers

There was a boy called Lee,
He drank loads of tea,
He liked playing conkers,
Which made him go bonkers,
And then he got stung by a bee.

Daniel Small (10)
Newtons Primary School, Rainham

Paul And The Wall

There was a young man called Paul,
Who climbed up a really big wall,
He had a cough
And then jumped off
And now he is really small.

Jennifer Harrad (9)
Newtons Primary School, Rainham

Poor Old Jack!

There was a young boy named Jack,
Who fell and broke his back,
Football no more
Back was sore
Now we all feel sorry for Jack.

Shannon Hemsley (9)
Newtons Primary School, Rainham

A Man Who Had A Flute

There was a man who had a flute
All the girls thought he was cute
When he started to play
All the girls ran away
As he started to take off his suit.

Charlie Davis (10)
Newtons Primary School, Rainham

A Boy From France

There was a boy from France
Who liked to dance and prance
His best friend was Luke
Who always used to puke
So now his best friend is Lance.

Jack Watson (10)
Newtons Primary School, Rainham

Jade Who Lived In A Bucket And Spade

There was a young girl called Jade
Who lived in a bucket and spade
She had a fat cat
With a bright red hat
But now she is best friends with the maid.

Jade Scanlan (9)
Newtons Primary School, Rainham

The Silly Inventor

There was a girl called Jill
Who invented a big yellow pill
It got stuck in her throat
And felt like a boat
So off she went home to chill.

Joanna Annett (10)
Newtons Primary School, Rainham

Mean Teacher

My teacher is not very nice
His hair is infested with lice
My mum complained
The teacher explained
And said he was not worth the price.

Ruth Adediran (9)
Newtons Primary School, Rainham

Gert The Mad Flirt

There was a girl called Gert
Who was a real big flirt
Bath always bubbling
Out always clubbing
And always getting badly hurt.

Hayley East (10)
Newtons Primary School, Rainham

Lance Goes To France

There was a young man called Lance
Who loved to do a lot of dance
He saw his friend Jack
And packed his backpack
And then sailed off to France.

Claire Potts (10)
Newtons Primary School, Rainham

Fat Pat

There once was a man named Pat
That was terribly, terribly fat
He went in a cave
He must have been brave
To squeeze through a tunnel like that.

Sophie Barton (9)
Newtons Primary School, Rainham

The Boy Who Walked Into A Wall!

There was a young man called Paul
Who walked into a very high wall
He flattened his face
Oh what a disgrace
And now he don't think he's all cool!

Georgina Poulton (10)
Newtons Primary School, Rainham

The Lady With A Daughter Called Sadie

There once was a big lady,
She had a daughter called Sadie,
She sat on a mat
And called herself fat,
That's the end of that lady.

Sophie Walker
Newtons Primary School, Rainham

Chelsea

C is for cat, playing with a shell.
H is for horse, that always smells.
E is for elephants that have big ears.
L is for Laurien, who always brings treats.
S is for swimming, go there every day.
E is for ears, they play and play.
A is for apple, that you eat!

Chelsea McDiarmaid (10)
Newtons Primary School, Rainham

Harry

H is for Harry, he's so nice
A is for ant, sometimes you find them in your rice
R is for rabbits, hopping around
R is for Robert he makes lots of sound
Y is for yellow, as bright as the sun

And my name is Harry and I have lots of fun.

Harry Nolan (10)
Newtons Primary School, Rainham

Daisy

D is for Daisy, she really is a pest
A is for apple, I think they are the best
I is for ice cream, vanilla's better than the rest
S is for snake, hissing in the nest
Y is for yawning, mustn't do it in the test.

Daisy Young (10)
Newtons Primary School, Rainham

Happiness

Happiness sounds like laughter
And chatting
Happiness smells like flowers when
I'm riding my bike in the park
Happiness feels like excitement running
Through my body
Happiness tastes like sweet cakes and candy!
Happiness looks like children playing with their friends.

Alexandra Grace (11)
Newtons Primary School, Rainham

The Environment

What can I hear?
I can hear birds singing in the morning, tweeting away.
Buses braking at the bus stop.
Children shouting with their friends on the way to school
Holding tight onto their books.

What can I feel?
I feel raindrops running down my face and me shaking off the
Coldness from outside.
I feel dark inside with no one around.
Now I feel happy that the clouds have cleared to let the sun
                                                come out.

What can I see?
I can see bees buzzing around a sunflower
Drinking the nectar off of the stigma.
I see people riding their bikes with their sunglasses
Because the sun is lighting up the Earth.

Elliot Scott (11)
Newtons Primary School, Rainham

The War

I can see pitch-black smoke storming out of blown-up buildings,
People dying in loneliness,
Soldiers like I protecting the innocents,
Our enemy wielding our dead for protection.

I can hear the screams of terrified people
Soldiers and others wailing in their last moments
The planes roaring their engine tired above me
Bombs exploding with a deafening bang.

I can feel my blood trickling down my skin,
Hatred from my enemy and teammates against each other
Bullets digging into my sore skin.

Jai Small (11)
Newtons Primary School, Rainham

War

What can you see?
I can see my poor man falling to the ground one by one.

What can you hear?
I can hear giant missiles aiming down on the homes
Of innocent people.

What do you feel like?
I feel like victory was soon here
But I had a feeling that it was my turn to die
And to fall into my heavenly sleep!
Goodbye! . . .

Jack Mercer (10)
Newtons Primary School, Rainham

War

What can you see?
Dead soldiers laying upon one another,
Injured soldiers crying in agony,
Bullets firing into soldiers,
Planes flying over my head causing planes to crash,
Tanks blowing through walls to victory.

What can you hear?
Screaming of injured soldiers,
Gunshots firing through the air,
Machine guns hammering into the enemy,
The war siren in the middle of an air raid,
The explosion of bombs and the fall of rubble.

What can you feel?
The tears streaming down my eyes,
For the ones which have been lost,
The blow of a bullet straight through my chest,
I can feel the pain of my body,
I can feel nothing anymore.

Frazer Collins (11)
Newtons Primary School, Rainham

What Is Green?

Green is grass
Getting greener and greener
Green is jealousy
It makes you feel meaner.

Green is mysterious
It makes you wonder
Green is lightning
And also for thunder.

Green is a grasshopper
With a knight's shield
Green is a butterfly
Fluttering across the field.

Green is lettuce
Planted in a farm
When you eat it
It brings you no harm.

James Cartwright (9)
Newtons Primary School, Rainham

Ancient Egypt

What can you see?
I can see gold all around me
And the tomb of the king covered in gold.

What can you hear?
I can hear rats and bats everywhere,
Spiders and flies as well.
The tomb of the mummy awakening.

What can you feel?
I feel like I'm a rich person for discovering the tomb.
I feel like a billionaire, famous too!

Katie Wong (11)
Newtons Primary School, Rainham

Ancient Egypt

What can you see?
Big, gold and glistening pyramids hung in the bright blue sky
With scary pharaohs with long zigzaggy hats
With strong velvet whips to whip the sad helpless slaves
With dark devil-red stripes down their back
Where they've been whipped.

What can you hear?
Slaves praying to God for Him to save them
And the howling of slaves shouting when they've got hit
By the mighty whip.
People crying when one of their family have died.

What can I feel?
Pain inside me like I am a poor slave getting whipped by terrifying
Pharaohs
Anger was rushing through me.
I want to take it out on the pharaohs
God was saying to me, 'Go stop the frightening slavery
Go kill all the pharaohs and feed the slaves for all they've been
through.'

Luke Scott (11)
Newtons Primary School, Rainham

Love

Love smells like a million roses thrown in the calm, gentle air.
Love sounds like my heart pounding up and down.
Love looks like a shooting star, while blasting off towards the sun.
Love tastes like a creamy, smooth chocolate, thrown in the air.
Love feels like red and pink hearts pounding around me
And it makes me feel warm inside.

Love is a romantic piece of art
Love looks like the red sky at sunset.

Jordan Collins (11)
Newtons Primary School, Rainham

The Samurai

What can you hear?
I can hear the clash of a warrior's blade
The clank clank of a samurai's armour
The galloping of horses' hooves
And the battle cry of a true warrior.

What can you feel?
I feel the presence of our monks in the temple
Focusing their chi and empowering on us to win the battle
I can feel the enemy's cowardliness
As I watch them flee across the plains.

What can you see?
I see a samurai blade swirling in the air
Before it smites down its victim
I see the blood of the enemy
Staining the ground
Yet in his death
I see victory for the samurai.

Albert Sherwood (11)
Newtons Primary School, Rainham

The Wasp

If I could,
See this wasp,
I would admire his beauty,
His buttercup yellow,
His cold charcoal black,
His wings are crispy wafers
He glides peacefully through the sky
Even his face
Is incredible
He breathes like me
He is like me!

Chelsey Chase (11)
Newtons Primary School, Rainham

War

What can you see?
Soldiers hurt on the floor in pain,
Evil bombs exploding
Machine guns lighting up the dark
Friends dying to death.

What can you hear?
People screaming
Machine guns lighting the sky without stopping
Houses falling down, people shouting,
Everything exploding.

What can you feel?
I can feel pain striking me
I can feel darkness in my heart
I can feel my ears exploding.

Kastriot Memeti (11)
Newtons Primary School, Rainham

Winter Winter!

Winter, winter! What a cold time!
When my ice cream melts all over my hands.

Winter, winter! What a cold time,
When I'm in my swimming suit
Swimming around in the sea.

Winter, winter! What a cold time!
When I'm sunbathing on the hot sand.

Winter, winter! What a cold time!
When I come in from school
Getting my summer dress on.

Winter, winter! What a cold time!
Isn't it?

Jade Gale (11)
Newtons Primary School, Rainham

What Is Green?

Green is the grass
Getting greener and greener
You might want to watch out
When it makes you meaner.

Grapes are green
Apples are too
These fruits are
Very good for you.

Green is mysterious
It makes you wonder
Like lightning
And thunder.

Green is a lettuce
Planted in the field
Green is mean
You might need a shield.

Rinna Ernstzen (8)
Newtons Primary School, Rainham

Love Love Love

Love feels like happiness in your heart and stays there forever.
Love smells like millions of red roses, that you can smell through
                                                                               the air.
Love tastes like chocolate shaped lovehearts that taste sweet.
Love looks like two pink lovehearts stuck together forever.
Love sounds like sweet romantic music playing in your ears.
I think love is beautiful and nothing can break it if you try
I think love is the world and nothing can take its place.

Chantel Dyer (11)
Newtons Primary School, Rainham

Boys Boys Boys!

Boys, boys with their fancy dresses,
    Boys, boys with their sparkling make-up
    Smeared over their faces,
Boys, boys with their nail varnish so clear and shimmering
    Boys, boys with their mascara on
    The colour of it as black as ebony
Boys, boys with the latest fashion high heel shoes
    Boys, boys with their miniskirts 10cm above their knees
    Frilly and bright
Boys, boys with their tiny little handbags
Swung gracefully over their shoulders with pride.
    Well I think they are.

Nancy Foley-Gannon (11)
Newtons Primary School, Rainham

It's Winter, It's Winter

It's winter, it's winter
The sun is blistering hot
It's winter, it's winter
As I jumped into the freezing pool
It's winter, it's winter
As I lick the dripping juice from the ice cold lolly
It's winter, it's winter
Everyone is scorching hot
It's winter, it's winter
As everyone is down at the warm noisy beach
It's winter, it's winter
Is it winter?

Jade Pattison (11)
Newtons Primary School, Rainham

Darkness

Darkness feels like a cold draft surrounding everything
Darkness smells like hot food going cold
Darkness sounds like an owl hooting all night
Darkness tastes like a drink growing mould
Darkness looks like the eclipse over the sun.

Kane Robertson (10)
Newtons Primary School, Rainham

A Bumblebee

If I could
See this bumblebee
With unprejudiced eye,
I should see his wing
Was pale blue
His mouth would make a buzzing sound
Annoyingly
I notice
And breathe as I do.

Roseline Mgbeike (11)
Newtons Primary School, Rainham

Goalkeepers

They dive and stretch
They grow big and tall
They go left and right
They go up and down
They go back and forth
They go in and out
Their hands are tools
They are goalkeepers.

Aaron Howard (8)
Newtons Primary School, Rainham

What Is Blue?

Blue is the colour
Of sadness
It can be bad
And full of madness.
Blue is the colour
Of bluebells
And also the colour
Of some seashells.
Blue is the colour
Of whales
In a blue, blue ocean
With boats with sails.
Blue is the colour
Of dolphins gliding by
And also bluebottles
Flying in the sky.

Taryn Harley (9)
Newtons Primary School, Rainham

Parents I Just Can't Stand Them!

Parents, I just can't stand them
When they get all their dinner around their face
Parents, I just can't stand them
When they kick footballs over the next-door neighbour's fence
Parents, I can't stand them
When they scoff themselves with sweets
Parents, I can't stand them
When they don't clear up their toys
Parents I can't stand them
When they just sit in front of the telly
Parents I just can't stand them!

Georgia Cunningham (10)
Newtons Primary School, Rainham

Favourite Seasons

My favourite season is autumn
I like to play outside
Rebecca's name is Marlton
I like to play on a slide
My favourite season is . . .

My favourite season is summer
I like to play on my mat
Everyone has a favourite number
I become a big cat
My favourite season is . . .

My favourite season is spring
I sit on my long
I jump like a great big king
I become a frog.
My favourite season is . . .

My favourite season is winter
I stay on my rug
My sweet has become minter
I drink from my best mug.
My favourite season is . . .

> *My favourites*
> *Are all the seasons!*

My favourite season is . . .
Gregoria Gati (8)
Newtons Primary School, Rainham

All About Wendy

There was an old lady called Wendy
And her legs were so terribly bendy
She went up a hill
And there she is still
And she thinks her legs are so trendy.
Taylor Thacker (8)
Newtons Primary School, Rainham

My Bedroom

A place to spend some time alone
A place I feel safe and can call it my own
A comfy bed surrounded by toys
A note on the door saying 'Keep out boys'
I can watch TV or play my music full blast
But when Mum comes in, I have to turn it down fast
As night-time falls I curl up in a ball
And fall asleep with no troubles at all.

Shannon Davis (9)
Newtons Primary School, Rainham

What Is Yellow?

Yellow is the feeling of happiness in the sky
Yellow makes you jump, skip and fly
Yellow is the sunshine all bright and hot
You will love the sound of yellow such a lot
It sounds like bells ringing all about
Yellow is something that makes you want to
Shout!

Risan Nishori (8)
Newtons Primary School, Rainham

White

White is the colour of relaxation
It makes you feel calm
And filled with happiness
It's the colour of a white fluffy cloud
It's so very quiet
Never loud
The colour is white
It makes me drift off to sleep
During the night.

Toby Cox (9)
Newtons Primary School, Rainham

Our Cat Jellicote

Jellicote was our black and white cat
She wasn't thin or fat
She'd wait at the door
Looking then scratching her paw.

Her eyes were big and yellow
She would lead and I would follow
In the garden along the path
Oops she fell in the old tin bath.

A bird lands on the grass
Jellicote pounces really fast
She missed her dinner
Our cat Jellicote is a winner.

Celine Franklin (9)
Newtons Primary School, Rainham

What Is Black?

Black is the loneliness
You feel when you are on your own
With no friends
And without a phone.

Black is the colour
Of deep rage
When you stamp your feet
In a rampage.

Black is the darkness
When you don't turn on the light
It's all around
In the middle of the night.

Charlotte Coleman (9)
Newtons Primary School, Rainham

What Is Blue?

Blue is the colour of the sky
Blue makes you feel that you're going to cry.

Blue is the colour of coldness
Oh no!
Blue is the colour of a pretty dodo!

Blue makes you feel very calm
Blue is the colour of a glossy lip balm.

Blue is the colour of thousands of whales
Blue is the colour of water in pails.

Blue is the colour when you're feeling sad
Blue is the colour when you're going mad.

Blue is the colour when you're feeling down
Blue is the colour when you're going to frown.

Blue is the colour when you're feeling hurt
Blue is the colour of a new T-shirt.

Ashlie East (8)
Newtons Primary School, Rainham

What Is Blue?

Blue is the colour
Of the sky
And the oceans
It's the colour of goodbye.

Blue is the colour
Of bluebells
Blue is the colour
Of strange smells.

Liam Renham (9)
Newtons Primary School, Rainham

Dark As Black

Black is the colour
Of no sign of life
It makes you feel
Like a husband without a wife.
It makes you feel
Lonely inside.
When you have nowhere to go
And just want to hide.
Black is the colour
Of a mystery
That is trying to be solved
Which will go down in history.

Black is the best colour.

Peace Ugbeikwu (9)
Newtons Primary School, Rainham

What Is Yellow?

Yellow is the sunshine shining bright
Yellow is the summer without a night
Yellow is happiness
All the way through
Yellow is the colour of chicken stew
Yellow is a fire burning hard
Yellow is the colour of my back yard
Children playing
All day long
Skipping, jumping, hopping
And singing a song.

Dafina Nishori (9)
Newtons Primary School, Rainham

Lauren

L is for Lauren, that's me and in the park, I like to play
A is for angel who shows me the way
U is for umbrella it keeps me dry
R is for robin flying high in the sky
E is for elephant he likes to scratch
N is for night-time when I watch a football match.

Lauren Smith (10)
Newtons Primary School, Rainham

What Is Orange?

Orange is the colour
Of excitement
It makes you want
To jump along the pavement.

Orange fills you
Up with happiness
It's the colour of a flame
The colour of hotness.

Jack Kennedy (9)
Newtons Primary School, Rainham

What Is Green?

Grass is green
So are the trees
It's also the colour
Of the summer breeze
It's the colour
Of grapes.

Joseph Hatcher (8)
Newtons Primary School, Rainham

Wendy

There once was a lady called Wendy
Her legs were terribly bendy
She tried to dance
And gave a glance
She found herself very trendy.

Nicole Painter (9)
Newtons Primary School, Rainham

Untitled

When life begins church bells ring
When a new baby is born,
Adults cheer whilst drinking their beer,
Loving and cuddling the new baby dear.

Your baby will start talking,
Soon it will be walking,
And growing a little more each day.

School comes and goes, years fly past,
Before you know it he will be married at last.
With a wife and children and a home of his own
The family circle begins again.
Hooray!

Jay Wyatt (10)
Newtons Primary School, Rainham

Anger

Anger is when a child is getting abused
Anger is when a man strikes a woman.
Anger is when your best friend walks away from you.
Anger is watching Man United lose at penalties
Against Arsenal.
Anger is when a baby dies.
That is what anger is to me.

Jack Ogbourne (11)
Rainham Village Primary School, Rainham

My Dog Beau

My dog Beau has a smelly toe
My dog can catch anything
As well as a crow
My dog goes woof
And people say shoosh!
So you better watch out for my Beau.

My dog Beau is fat I suppose
What's bad about her is her toes
They smell of rotten cheese, cor!
They've got to go
So be careful with my Beau.

My dog Beau is scared of hamsters
My dog Beau doesn't wear Pampers
My dog Beau is the best dog I've ever known,
That's all about my Beau.

But there's one more thing about her
She loves her biscuits and her kisses
That should be everything about my dog Beau!

Nicole Gregory (10)
Rainham Village Primary School, Rainham

Emotions

Anger is Manchester United losing to Arsenal
                                        on penalties.

Anger is when I get loads of homework.

Happiness is getting a new wrestler.

Happiness is having a cool Dr Pepper on a hot day.

Sadness is when I get beaten up.

Sadness is when a member of my family dies.

Sam Harber (11)
Rainham Village Primary School, Rainham

What Am I?

I have no colour,
Not even white,
But sometimes I'm wide
And blue.

Sometimes I'm still
And sometimes I rush,
And sometimes I'm in
Things that are new!

It's hard to hold me,
I cool you down
But without me you
Couldn't live.

You can control me.

This poem is a secret,
Never to be told!

Daisy Cook (11)
Rainham Village Primary School, Rainham

Are Fairies True?

Are fairies true?
Fluttering around with nothing to do
You can only see them at night so don't lose your sight
With pretty pink dresses and ballerina shoes.

What can we do?
What can we do?
Can you hear them at night
With their shiny, shiny wings
And their little voices
And all their different choices
Of different clothes.

I wonder if they're real.

Abbie Carter (9)
Rainham Village Primary School, Rainham

The Open Door
(Based on 'The Door' by Miroslav Holub)

Open the door
What can you see?
A tropical beach
With a glittering sea.

Open the door
What can you see?
Maybe there's diamonds
Shimmering in the scarlet sun.

Open the door
What can you see?
Is there a gentle bee
Crossing the leaf?

Open the door
Even if it's just the howling wind
Dancing with the trees . . .

Dean Brunt (8)
Rainham Village Primary School, Rainham

My Mum

My mum is the best,
She cleans and cooks,
My mum is never in a mess,
She reads books.

My mum has short, red, string hair,
Rose-red cheeks,
She is always fair,
She tells me I'm cheeky!

She gives me hugs and kisses
She is always caring,
If I go away she misses me,
She's always there with me,
I hope she never dies.

Samantha Sommerville (8)
Rainham Village Primary School, Rainham

Go Open The Door
(Based on 'The Door' by Miroslav Holub)

Go open the door,
Maybe there's a lake with a golden swan sitting on the surface.

Go further through the door,
Maybe there's the moon watching over the glistening stars,
And the fairies dancing by the moonlight.

Go even further through the door,
Can you see the mermaid sitting on the rocks
Look at her blonde, long, smooth hair
And her tail in the sun
Look, it's changing from the colour silver to gold.

Go to the end of the door
Can you see a pot of gold waiting patiently for you
To pick it up at the end of a rainbow.

Annie Boxer (9)
Rainham Village Primary School, Rainham

Soldier At War

The sight of people holding a bazooka with fright
A man wounded by machine guns shooting continuously
Then with air bombs coming from planets destroying hundreds
The men huddled in the corner frantically holding guns.

The sound of shotguns and air guns firing in the air
The sound also of six marines saving you from death
The sound of sorrowful people crying from guns.

The feel of dirt breaking down gradually on your neck
The feel that you have a gun at your head but it is your imagination
The feel also of darting and dodging enemy fire.

Arron Bernard (9)
Rainham Village Primary School, Rainham

My Feelings

Helplessness is Manchester United losing
Helplessness is someone dying
Helplessness is my mother and father continuously arguing.

Fear is my parents dying
Fear is when I don't get the highest level
Fear is with a capital F.

Jealousy is when my sole friend finds another close friend
Jealousy is when someone else has something better than me,
Jealousy is when I get less attention.

Sarah Aramide (11)
Rainham Village Primary School, Rainham

Karate

What can you see?
I can see children dressed in white,
With multicoloured belts.

I can see children doing kata
Combinations and pair techniques

What can you feel?
I can feel me tensing up when
I am asked to do a punch.

I can feel the strength in me

What can you hear?
I can hear children kicking
And shouting pinanedan.

I can hear the sensei saying instructions
And telling them what to do.

Tyler Roberts (9)
Rainham Village Primary School, Rainham

Food At McDonald's

I would like a Big Mac
But could it make me fat?
Oh well, it is too late for that,
I've ordered it now.
It's only a snack,
I might need a Tic-Tac.

Yay, it has finally come,
My friends say the consequence is a ton.
It's only beef in a bun
And really good fun.
I must say it is worth a ten mile run.

I must sink my teeth
Into that succulent beef,
Me and my friends
Say it's really neat.

I must have it again,
Again and again,
I must have it again
And with succulent fat.

Oh my goodness,
I'm going insane!

Charles Hall (10)
Rainham Village Primary School, Rainham

The Sun

I am the sun
I am like the hot burning intensity of a thousand fires,
I am like a big tin can of brightly coloured paint
Like red, orange and yellow,
I am like a calm fire lying on the grass of a campsite
With beautiful shining stars in the sparkling blue night sky,
I am like a yellow towel wrapped round a body on a warm
                                              evening at the beach.

Katie Nelson (9)
Rainham Village Primary School, Rainham

My Best Friend

My best friend is so cool,
He's a bit weird and so small,
He likes watching The Simpsons,
In my 50 foot pool!

We have known each other for quite some time,
He hates the Prime Minister, Tony Blair's guts,
He is the prime person in our gang,
As he knows he's number one!

His nickname is devil dare James
He will do anything you say,
He's also got a friend called Mr Neville
He also wears gold and talks about rebels
Bling! Bling! I hear him call,
As my mum just put the car on stall.

James is a gangster,
He is a bad boy which is so good,
He is one of us in the gangster 'hood',
Which means bad news for people who live there,
Him and I could take on one of those polar bears.

I've had enough,
I'll take no more,
In one minute,
I'll get James on the floor,
Because he bothered me while I was writing,
I'm out of here because I'm going hiking.

Robert Park (10)
Rainham Village Primary School, Rainham

A Child In The Playground

There are many children on the playground,
Playing with balls, skipping ropes and bats.
Lots of friends on the playground,
Some are not friends.

Aliyah Park (7)
Rainham Village Primary School, Rainham

Arsenal Are Champs

A is for absolutely great
R ivals crying
S upport Arsenal
E is for Edu scoring
N o one gets past Lehmann
A ngry rivals
L ovely goal by Henry

A rsenal are the best
R the reds winning?
E motional fans

C hampions again
H enry scoring like always
A lways winning
M en playing football
P layers scoring
S o many goals.

Michael Busby (10)
Rainham Village Primary School, Rainham

Soldier

Sweat was rolling down my face
The gunfire was coming closer
Nearer and nearer it crept
To take many of our lives
The only thing that we could do
Is fight for our lives.

We fought for many hours
Wishing we were at home
Even though we had strength
They overpowered us
We fled to a safe distance
And called for help
Help never arrived, we were alone
Now lost in time, *forever.*

John Beth (11)
Rainham Village Primary School, Rainham

Family Life

Dad's tall
Mum's small
Sister annoying
Brother boring
Dog going mental
Cat going strange
Mouse is trying to get out the cage
Fish swimming round, nobody cares
My baby rats are growing hair.

I guess I have to stay in my room
Writing and playing right through till noon
Trying to ignore my sister's crying
Trust me, really I am trying!
School project due tomorrow
Not done yet, I am getting sorrow
Got to write a poem, better get going.

Mum is pregnant, yippee . . . not
Another baby to wipe snot
On furniture and clothes, I am hiding all mine
Oh no! Got to go now, it is time.

Zoe Elsmore (10)
Rainham Village Primary School, Rainham

Inner

The emotion crashes like a wave
Then simmers like a never-ending day
My beloved pain sinks deep inside
It is a betrayed portrait I cannot hide
The fire burns with a cold freeze
The inner emotion brings a hated breeze
I sit here drowning in my own tears
Facing . . . my hardest fears.

Stephanie Lovett (10)
Rainham Village Primary School, Rainham

My Dog Smells Like . . .

My dog smells like rotten cheese,
My dog smells like dead fleas,
My dog smells like lifeless fish
Fried in a cooking dish.

My dog smells like out of date eggs
My dog smells like bedbugs in my bed
My dog smells like skunk pong!
And a few pieces of bull's dung!

My dog smells like rabbit droppings
My dog smells like someone hasn't been bathing
My dog smells like birds bombing
Also the expiry date of milk coming.

My dog smells like rubbish in a dump
My dog smells like earwax building up to a heap,
My dog smells like junk and garbage
Oh I wish he would take a bath – I wish, I wish . . .

Abiola Ricketts (10)
Rainham Village Primary School, Rainham

Warriors At War

Through the dismal, mulching weeds
We travel cautiously.

Creepily crouching through the moor
Enemy is not far right now.

Firing bullets spurring near,
We travel through without breaking fear

Enemy turrets close by men by the bombs blazing

Yet together we stand not as soldiers but
As brothers, we shall prevail.

Olivia Ibanez-Solano (11)
Rainham Village Primary School, Rainham

Dead

The phone stops,
Everything is still,
Not a movement,
Not a sound.

The chill of the night,
No one in sight,
Not even a dog,
Not a sound is made.

The trickle of blood,
From his head,
The murder weapon,
Just waiting to be found.

The sorrow of the night,
People upset,
Now there's a sound,
A siren,
All flashing and blue.

Kirsty Lake (11)
Rainham Village Primary School, Rainham

A Soldier At War

In a fierce force field
Tired men, people perishing
Lives perishing
Bazooka's exploding
Machine guns hammering
Shotguns banging
Rain falling
Burning
Blood spurting.

Joseph Smyth (8)
Rainham Village Primary School, Rainham

I Asked A Little Boy If He Could See

I asked a little boy if he could see.
The boy said, 'No, why can you see me?'
I said, 'Can you see the blue colours in the sky?'
He said, 'No, why?'
I said, 'Can you see the green of the grass?'
He said, 'No, why do you ask?'
I said, 'Can you see the yellow of the sun?'
He said, 'No, what has it done?'
I said, 'Can you see the white colours of the clouds?'
He said, 'No why, are they loud?'
I said, 'Can you see the different colours in the rainbow?'
He said, 'No why, is it a beautiful show?'
'Well, how do you see?
How do you know the colours as they shine and glow without vision?
How sad!'
He looked at me and said with a smile,
'My feelings tell me all that I need to see,
So don't be sad,
It isn't that bad!'

Joanne Price (10)
Rainham Village Primary School, Rainham

A Soldier At War

On the field there are many people dying
Machine guns going off
Bombs are exploding and people were on fire
I saw something
A person on my side killed the leader.
You can hear bombs and machine guns going off
You can feel guns in your hand
You can feel the rain.

Samuel Wood (8)
Rainham Village Primary School, Rainham

Things

I see lovely flowers waving in the air,
I see grasshoppers jumping like they just don't care,
I see grass bouncing up and down,
I see rabbits jumping up off the ground,
I see lots of things.

I feel grass from the lovely ground,
I feel sparkling water glistening in the sun,
I feel smooth flower petals soft and warm,
I feel nice and cool bathing in the moon,
I feel lots of things.

Lucy Ramsey (8)
Rainham Village Primary School, Rainham

Seasons

It's wintertime for fun and play
Everyone's hiding while snowballs are flying
Through the snowy dark sky.

It's spring
Winter has ended.
Children crying, adults cheering as cold passes on,
Flowers shooting up.
Park's filling up as heat goes on.

It's summer
Beaches full as children pass through
Children splash in the animal-infested blue sea.

It's autumn
Leaves falling off trees
Coloured leaves everywhere.

Robert-Lee Hall (8)
Rainham Village Primary School, Rainham

Horses Racing

I can see flags waving up and down
I can see riders nervously step onto their horses
I can see crowds of people jumping up and down
I can see horses jumping carefully
I can see horses racing up and down.

I can feel the wind in my face
I can feel the furry horses
I can feel the sand on the racetrack
I can feel the raindrops
I can feel the coldness on my hands.

I can hear horses' hooves
I can hear people cheering
I can hear people screaming
I can hear horses neighing
I can hear cars on the road.

Danielle Beavis (8)
Rainham Village Primary School, Rainham

Home Compared To Tsunami

You're probably listening to the bells ringing at home,
There's me listening to babies screaming and dying.
It's probably quiet and peaceful at home,
But here there's shouting, screaming and more.

You're probably waiting for Santa to come,
There's me waiting for people to come and to save others.

You're waiting for presents to come from Santa,
There's me seeing coffins being passed around.
So that's home compared to Tsunami.

Elizabeth Miller (10)
Rainham Village Primary School, Rainham

Never-Ending

The war ends with blood everywhere
But who said it's over, there is more wars to come
So now I think about it, it makes me glum
I wonder why we have wars, it's dumb.

Coffins coming by
It makes me cry
Friends and family dead
While I lay in bed.

I feel so ashamed
Because I play my games
I miss my family
At night I am sad.

Will this war never end?

Deanna Gammans (9)
Rainham Village Primary School, Rainham

Home Compared To Iraq

At home I would watch telly, play on the computer or listen to music,
But in war I don't even sleep.
At home I go to the local swimming pool and go in deep,
But the water supply in Iraq is very short and the food is the
                                                          same sort.
Defending my body, my life, my hair, well that is my life,
As I sit in a tank with a rifle and knife,
I will be home soon, I promise, with a medal
And I have made a silly song called 'I am a Rebel'.
When I come back it could make millions,
One day I could own a mansion worth billions
And I would put it in Rainham because it's home.

Christopher Thompson (10)
Rainham Village Primary School, Rainham

The Beautiful Flower

The flower is so pretty
It lives in the garden nearby the city,
Flowers are colourful,
And they are wonderful.

Oh flower why you smell,
I will call you Bluebell
Oh my flower,
You take to grow an hour.

Flower needs sunshine
So it will grow fine
And flower needs water
Oh you're growing.

You grow so fast
Finally at last!

Joanna Guzman (10)
Rainham Village Primary School, Rainham

Anger Or Happiness?

Anger is with a capital A,
Anger is watching your best friend go away,
Anger is watching a hungry, lonely baby cry,
Anger is losing a football match,
Anger is with a capital A.

Happiness is with a special capital H,
Happiness is watching a healthy baby live,
Happiness is winning a football match,
Happiness is watching my best friend stay,
No one can be happier than me!

Jasleen Bhogal (11)
Rainham Village Primary School, Rainham

I Got Beat Up

I got beat up, beat up,
I wish I did not, did not,
I hope it doesn't happen again I hope, I hope, I hope

They are waiting for me at lunchtime, so they can
Flush my head down the toilet, for a third time.

I got beat up, beat up
I wish I did not, did not,
I hope it doesn't happen I hope, I hope, I hope.

What shall I do, what can I do, hide in the dustbin
Or skip school where I am treated so cruel?

I got beat up, beat up,
I wish I did not, did not
I hope it doesn't happen again, I hope, I hope, I hope.

I've lost a tooth, I've got a black eye
I think I'm going to cry
I wish bullies didn't exist
I've got to learn to resist.

I got beat up, beat up
I wish I did not, I did not
I hope it doesn't happen again, I hope, I hope, I hope.

Stand up for myself
Use my brain that will help

As my mum always says
The word is mightier than the sword!

Teal Anderson (10)
Rainham Village Primary School, Rainham

A Butterfly

A butterfly may flutter by
See a shimmer of a dragonfly.
It is summertime
And the living can be seen.
In the orchard green.
It is a crazy thing
The song I hear, in the orchard green.

Jasdeep Nijjar (8)
Rainham Village Primary School, Rainham

Passed Away

The tears trickled down my face,
My red, puffy, sore eyes,
My heart felt like it had been stabbed
Twelve times and left to bleed,
Lying there on my own
Knowing I will never see him again,
My life froze the day my grandad died!

Hayley Kitt (10)
Rainham Village Primary School, Rainham

I Am Happy

I am happy when West Ham win,
I am happy at home,
I am happy when my favourite food is cooked,
I am happy when something good is on TV,
I am happy when I play football,
Most of all,
I would be the happiest person if school did not exist!

Sarah Beeson (10)
Rainham Village Primary School, Rainham

My Fear

My fear is like a drop of dragon's blood
My fear is like the fear of a green-eyed, black cat
My fear is like a snake being swallowed by a one-eyed monster
My fear is like the headless Frankenstein stabbing me to death
My fear, my fear is like a vampire biting my neck
My fear is like the black coal melting in the sun
My fear is like the snake gripping onto Amie's head
And seeing blood dripping from her neck
My fear never goes away
My fear is just not fair
My fear is as terrifying as a black cat
Caught in the middle of a dark road
Trapped in the glare of the monster with the beaming headlights
Fear
    Fear
        Fear
            My fear.

Fatmata Jah (10)
Rainham Village Primary School, Rainham

What Makes Me Angry

It makes me angry when West Ham lose,
It makes me angry when nobody listens to me,
It makes me angry when my food is burnt,
It makes me angry when my football team loses,
It makes me angry when my mum goes away,
It makes me angry when my brother picks on me,
It makes me angry when people call me names,
It makes me angry when we don't have a lot of PE,
The thing that makes me angriest is when nobody plays with me.

Sarah Skipper (11)
Rainham Village Primary School, Rainham

My Worst Nightmare

One day I came home from school
Mum and Dad had gone
All they left was a set of rules.
I froze
Never had something like this happened
A shiver ran up my spine
My day turned from good to bad
My worst nightmare had come to life.

I sat on the sofa, weeping
Where had they gone?
I phoned my relatives
But just to find more despair . . .
They had disappeared
For my worst nightmare had truly come to life.

Adam Challis (11)
Rainham Village Primary School, Rainham

Soldiers In The War

I would like to be a soldier in the war,
I have imagined it a million times before,
They have to be honoured,
Otherwise there is no point in saving our lives.

In the war, people live, people die,
No one gets to say goodbye,
They go to a place where no one knows,
But still, everyone goes.

They go to save us,
Their lives are at risk.

Thomas Tyrrell (11)
Rainham Village Primary School, Rainham

Live And Die

People live, people die,
Most of us don't get to say goodbye.
It's a natural thing when people go,
To the place that we don't know.

The people in your family can't always stay,
Sooner or later they'll pass away.
Try not to make them stay too long,
Because then you'll hear their funeral song.

It's a sad thing when your loved ones die
And you'll be left with just a sigh.

Katherine Rodwell (11)
Rainham Village Primary School, Rainham

A Soldier

Fear, worry, hung in the air,
Black smoke everywhere.

A soldier looking at his loved ones,
As he prepares himself for battle.

The feeling of his fellow soldier,
As he lures himself helplessly into a trap,
As he sees him being blown up like a rat.

Oh, how he wishes he had stayed at home,
Kent is a wonderful, posh place,
He wonders how he made this choice.

But he knows he came here to die,
But wanted to say his last goodbye.

Philip Modu (10)
Rainham Village Primary School, Rainham

Fear

Fear is frightening,
I can hear it in my room,
I hear ghosts screaming
And I hear doors creaking.

I see blood on the walls
And down in the halls,
There are eyeballs looking at me
And trying to knock my tea.

The owls are making a noise
And who is moving my toys?
The room is pitch-black,
As something climbs on my back.

Thump! Thump! Thump!
Oh, what is that?

Chloe Hemmett Fuller (9)
Rainham Village Primary School, Rainham

An Apple Tree In The Summer

An apple tree in the summer,
People pick apples off the tree,
They smell, they see as they eat the lovely juicy apple,
What colour apples do you like?
I like red apples and green apples,
Green, juicy apples are the best, yum-yum,
Apples juicy, green and tasty . . .mmm,
Crunchy apples off the summer apple tree,
I just can't stop picking them and eating them,
An apple tree in summer!

Lynsey Coleman (11)
Rainham Village Primary School, Rainham

I'm Bowling It

It's me thunder,
I will knock you six feet under,
No wonder, I will hit you with my thunder,
I'm bowling it down the street,
10,000mph
With my bottom up
And I've got a paper cut,
Nothing to do about it,
Don't give me your lip,
Or you are going to get ripped,
People call me prankster,
But I think I am a gangster,
This girl agrees with me,
So I need to thank her,
I am rolling down the street,
This is so neat - I'm bowling it!

James Lofty (10)
Rainham Village Primary School, Rainham

My Grumpy Sister!

My grumpy sister has dark brown eyes,
When my grumpy sister gets angry she starts a strop
And gets an attitude towards me,
Her eyes start to go all red, like rubies,
When she gets angry she stamps her feet really hard on the ground,
When she gets in the car she slams the door,
If she gets angry she fights with me upstairs,
Every time my grumpy sister gets angry she puts on a face
                                                                       like thunder,
My grumpy sister is called Louise.

Katherine Wisbey (11)
Rainham Village Primary School, Rainham

Fear

When the bullet
Was fired from the gun
Fear was my main element.

As it came straight at me
It flew at 200mph
In the blink of an eye.

With a wham and a bam
It smashed the telephone box
But it fired again.

I felt something
Trickle down my leg
It was . . . *blood!*

Jonathan Hime (10)
Rainham Village Primary School, Rainham

It's Summer, It's Summer

It's summer, it's summer,
When children have smoothies.
It's summer, it's summer,
When people go swimming
In the shimmering water.
It's summer, it's summer,
When the sand is in people's feet.
It's summer, it's summer,
When flowers start to bloom.
It's summer, it's summer,
When adults have glittery bikinis on.
It's summer, it's summer!

Nikita Ghataura (8)
Rainham Village Primary School, Rainham

The Important Thing Of Rugby

Men kick me
Men grab me
Men take me
Men tab me

The audience swear
The audience fight
The audience cheer
The audience non bright

This is me
I'm the ball
Rugby is an important thing
The most important thing of all.

Gareth Beth (9)
Rainham Village Primary School, Rainham

Darkness

Darkness is scary, darkness is lairy
Darkness is in the forest
Darkness is my devil
Darkness is in the classroom,
The bullies will never go away
Darkness is my fear
Darkness is everywhere
Ugly
Scary
Evil
Terrifying
Frightening
Sickening
Darkness!

Michael Olaribigbe (10)
Rainham Village Primary School, Rainham

What Should We Do With A Lazy Teacher?

What should we do with a lazy teacher?
What should we do with a lazy teacher?
What should we do with a lazy teacher?
Early in the morning.
Pin her to a bed while she's eating,
Tie her up while she's still sleeping.
'Please Miss, get up, please.
Miss, you've been in bed for almost two hours.
Do I need magic powers?'
What should we do with a lazy teacher?
What should we do with a lazy teacher?
What should we do with a lazy teacher?
Early in the morning.
Tickle her toes while she is sleeping,
Buy her a box of itching powder,
Turn on the TV louder,
Early in the morning.
'Why don't you get up, lazy teacher?
We need to do some learning, teacher,
Early in the morning.
We need to learn our ABCs
We need to learn our 1, 2, 3s.
So stop the *zzzzzs*
Early in the morning.'

Lauren Ginn (10)
Rainham Village Primary School, Rainham

A Soldier At War

The soldiers can see everyone dying,
The soldiers can hear people screaming, 'Help, I am dying.'
We soldiers think we are going to die, but we have to be brave.
Bombs exploding, killing millions,
Soldiers get so scared that they pretend to die.

Scott Coghlan (8)
Rainham Village Primary School, Rainham

A Tree In A Forest

A tree in a forest,
It's as tall as a giant,
As sturdy as a rock.

A tree in a forest,
It's as thin as a sheet of paper,
But as strong as a gorilla.

A tree in a forest,
Has as many arms as a spider,
The arms are the branches and they are very strong,
As strong as an ox.

A tree in a forest,
Is no longer there,
It has been chopped down like the others.

A tree in a forest,
Will live again,
Maybe it is now this paper.

Melissa Hunt (9)
Rainham Village Primary School, Rainham

A School Bus On Its Way To School

The children are being deafening
They are very enthusiastic
They are shrieking and yelling
They are ready for school

Now they are off the bus
It is glorious and silent
While I am waiting
I'll take a nap. *Zzzzzz!*

Emma McCloud (9)
Rainham Village Primary School, Rainham

A Monster Under My Bed

There's a monster under my bed!
I'm sure, I'm sure.
With two beady eyes and ten sharp claws,
Mum, there's a monster under my bed!
I'm sure, I'm sure.
With two bushy eyebrows and he's dribbling on the floor,
Dad, there's a monster under my bed!
I'm sure, I'm sure.
Dad, is it against the law?
I don't know.
The monster just ignores.
Gran, there's a monster under my bed!
I'm sure, I'm sure.
It's clutching onto my ankle,
It's going to drag me onto the floor!
Quick everybody, save yourself!
It's dragging me down to the Underworld.
That monster under my bed!

Kayleigh Saunter (9)
Rainham Village Primary School, Rainham

Water

Water can be cold,
Water can be hot,
Water can be frozen,
Water can be drunk,
Water can clean things,
Water can be poured,
Water is everywhere.

What would we do without water?

Marvyn Ashton (10)
Rainham Village Primary School, Rainham

Wrestling With Dad, Ouch!

Dad said, 'Be a man and let's fight.'
I said, 'Please Dad, not tonight.'
Anyway, he traps me! Grabs me!
Twists and crabs me,
Military presses me,
Jackhammers me,
Tombstones me,
Bear hugs me,
(He thinks he's Booker-T),
Chops me,
Sharp shooters me.
'Submit, son.'
'No!'
Chokes me,
Dragon screws me.
'Dad, why are you doing this to me?
Mum, help!'
Mum's busy making tea,
Dad sneak attacks me,
Body slams me,
Forearm smashes me,
Black widows me,
Cross-faces me,
Diving headbutts me,
Choke slams me,
Scoop slams me,
1,
2,
3,
Fall.
'Now what did you do at school?'

Awais Butt (10)
Rainham Village Primary School, Rainham

A Child In The Playground

If I was a child in the playground,
I could carefully see people playing,
People grabbing games
And people trying to concentrate on writing.

If I was a child in the playground,
I could hear people crying,
I could hear the annoying swing creaking
And people whistling.

If I was a child in the playground,
I could feel the wind touching me,
I could feel someone tapping me,
I could feel people enjoying themselves,
Just like how I feel.

Kelly Mavididi (9)
Rainham Village Primary School, Rainham

Gymnastics Ribbon

I can see pretty girls leaping, jumping and whirling in all they do
And then it's my go, I get swung about like they don't care,
I never get a glimpse of the beautiful shapes.

All I feel is a tight grip,
I feel air blowing through my hair,
I can feel wooden floorboards on my back.

I can hear soft thumping,
I can hear swooshing,
I can hear springs,
I can hear crinkling,
I can hear jumping.

Amie Cook (8)
Rainham Village Primary School, Rainham

A Rugby Ball

I can see people grabbing me,
I can see people throwing me,
I can see people watching me,
I can see people staring at me,
I can hear people cheering.

Zachary Pearce (9)
Rainham Village Primary School, Rainham

A Rainy Day

A rainy day is a dark, cold basement
A rainy day is a dark pool of water
A rainy day is a dark cavern
A rainy day is a dark, cold cupboard
That has never been opened
A rainy day is a dark box
That always stays shut.

Kayla Nielsen (11)
Riverside Middle School, Mildenhall

William Wallace

He is like the strongest bagpipe, louder than all others.
He is like a cat, landing on four feet.
He is like water that puts out all fire.
He is like a blizzard, knocking you back every time you try again.

Oliver Smith (10)
Riverside Middle School, Mildenhall

Old Granny Vera

She is like a harp, music to your ears
She is like an oak tree, very stiff and strong
She is like a fire, always glowing
She is like a snowstorm, pale and soft.

Harry Clark (9)
Riverside Middle School, Mildenhall

50 Cent

He
is like a rock,
big and hard,
loud and powerful.
He is like a bear,
fierce and mean.
He is like a fist,
for picking a fight.
He is like the shade,
blocking the light.

Keyarno Curtis (9)
Riverside Middle School, Mildenhall

Mum

She is like the beautiful sound of a piano.
She is like a daffodil, always smiling in the sun.
She is like the sand sparkling in the sun.
She is like a snowflake, as pretty as can be.

Melissa Jackson (10)
Riverside Middle School, Mildenhall

Jim Carrey

He is like a trumpet breaking into pieces
He is like a goat going crazy
He is like fire burning into flames
He is like the sun of the world.

Joshua Feltner (9)
Riverside Middle School, Mildenhall

Wayne Rooney

He is like a bass drum as he runs
And the ground shakes.
He runs like a cheetah
That's catching its food.
He is like a bit of fire spreading fast
As he runs with shining shoes.
He is like the wind
Because he's so fast with the ball.

Luke Ames (10)
Riverside Middle School, Mildenhall

George

He is like a violin,
He is small and makes a high-pitched sound.
He is like a twig, fragile.
He is like fire when he gets angry.
He is like a sunny day, always smiling.

Chris Barton (10)
Riverside Middle School, Mildenhall

St Jimmy

He is like an electric guitar that rocks the world,
He is like a leopard that can roll like the wind,
St Jimmy is like fire that burns everything,
He is like lightning that will strike the radio in fame.

Curtis Cronin (10)
Riverside Middle School, Mildenhall

Michael Owen

He is like a drum when his feet hit the ground
He is like a ball raring to go
He is like the sun, red-hot and ready to play
He is like thunder when he hits the football into the top
                                            left-hand corner.

Harry Leonard (9)
Riverside Middle School, Mildenhall

Nedved

He is like a drumbeat running down the field,
He is like a cheetah because he runs so fast,
He is like a fire burning down the field,
He is like a storm striking down the players.

Edward Pooley (9)
Riverside Middle School, Mildenhall

Cristiano Ronaldo

He is like a guitar as he does his tricks.
He is like a cheetah as he runs through the wind.
He is like the water as he rushes towards the goal.
He is like the wind as he skips past everybody.

Sam Davis (10)
Riverside Middle School, Mildenhall

Arnold Schwartzenegger

He is like an electric guitar with his treacherous voice.
He is like a black panther with his huge muscles.
He is like a waterfall crashing with his footsteps.
He is like a treacherous thunderstorm.

Martin Shaw (10)
Riverside Middle School, Mildenhall

All The People In My School

My English teacher is a shining star,
She is hanging in the sky, shining at night.
My best friend is a glittering guitar,
I play with her day and night.
All the people are elves grinning from ear to ear.
The person I sit next to is a beautiful old lady,
She talks to me every minute of the day.
My form teacher is a fiery dragon,
He fires at everyone during the day.

Keturah Cumber (10)
Riverside Middle School, Mildenhall

Elvis

He is like a guitar rocking his heart out.
He is like a dog howling on a stage.
He is like fire blazing on a stage.
His fingers move like the wind
Plucking his guitar strings.

Jay Sharp (10)
Riverside Middle School, Mildenhall

Dan

He is like a crocodile creeping through the water.
He is like a drum beating on the ground.
He is like a dragon breathing on a house.

Charlotte Baker (9)
Riverside Middle School, Mildenhall

Henry VIII

He is like a bull charging through a village.
He is like a drum banging people out of his way.
He is like a fire that burns down towns.
He is like a blizzard freezing people in their tracks.

Elliott Langham (10)
Riverside Middle School, Mildenhall

Manchester United

They are like a violin because they play like one.
They are like a tiger because they run as fast as one.
They are like fire because they are sometimes dirty.
They are like a blizzard because they're in one place,
Then they're in another.

Amy Flack (10)
Riverside Middle School, Mildenhall

Nanny

She is like a harp, as gentle as the sound of a harp.
She is a mouse, as quiet as a mouse.
She is like the water that is so calm.
She is like the sun so people can see her.

Haleigh Bragg (9)
Riverside Middle School, Mildenhall

Michael Owen

He is a bass drum when he runs and makes an earthquake.
He is a dandelion, so bendy when he scores a goal.
He is the speed of light when he runs.
He is a thunderbolt that shatters the world.

Alex Goodenough (10)
Riverside Middle School, Mildenhall

Adam Tilbrook

He is a drum because he is so loud
He is a tree because he is so tall
He is a sun because he is so bright
He is the lightning because he runs so fast.

Ashleigh Tilbrook (10)
Riverside Middle School, Mildenhall

Frank Lampard

He is like a drum that shakes the turf.
He is like a turtle who doesn't get hurt.
He is like a fire that flickers round the stadium.
He is like thunder that beats the goalie.

Sean Hebb (10)
Riverside Middle School, Mildenhall

Snail

A friendly, frightened garden stealer
A slow, sleeping movement maker
A one-footed slimy shifter
A heavy- shelled home lifter
A crunchy, crushed short liver
I'm a . . .

Leah Patterson (8)
Rose Hill Primary School, Ipswich

The Mini-Beast Hunt

I should love to see the fragrant flowers in the tall grass,
I should like to hear the beautiful butterfly when I'm looking
                                          for mini-beasts,
I should like to touch the slimy snail on the log and feel its shell,
I should like to take home a bird's white feather and paint its
                                                     tiny fleas,
I should like to understand why a butterfly has such
                                      symmetrical wings.

Louise Harling (7)
Rose Hill Primary School, Ipswich

A Bug Watch

I should like to see the colourful butterfly in the flower,
I should like to hear the buzzing bee when I'm looking up
                                                at the sky,
I should like to touch the smooth wood of the fence and feel
                                            the sharp points,
I should like to take home a slimy snail and paint its brown
                                          shell multicoloured,
I should like to understand why bees collect nectar.

George Bemrose (7)
Rose Hill Primary School, Ipswich

An Environmental Walk

I should like to see the fragrant flowers under a tree,
I should like to hear the humming of the bees when I'm looking
                                              at a flower,
I should like to touch the flickering grass of the ground and feel
                                              that it is dry,
I should like to take home a wiggly woodlouse and paint its firm back,
I should like to understand what a worm likes to eat.

Kai Hardy (7)
Rose Hill Primary School, Ipswich

A Bug Hunt

I should like to see the delicate butterfly on a grassy field,
I should like to hear the buzzing bee when I'm feeling really happy,
I should like to touch the fragile petals of the poppy and feel its
                                                                                               hairy stem,
I should like to take home a fluffy bird and paint its tiny head,
I should like to understand how a caterpillar can make a cocoon
And turn into a butterfly.

Esther Howard (7)
Rose Hill Primary School, Ipswich

A Bug Walk

I should like to see the refreshing flower by the tree,
I should like to hear the singing birds when I'm feeling very sad,
I should like to touch the hard wood of the bench and feel the
                                                                                               bumpy legs,
I should like to take home a beautiful butterfly and paint its
                                                                                           yellow wings,
I should like to understand why a spider spins a web.

Harrison Smith (7)
Rose Hill Primary School, Ipswich

Bugs

I should like to see the bright bee on the damp tree,
I should like to hear the tweeting birds when I'm under the grey sky,
I should like to touch the bumpy bark of the tree and feel
                                                                                              its branches,
I should like to take home a squiggling snail and paint its boring shell,
I should like to understand how a spider spins its web.

Benjamin Kersey (7)
Rose Hill Primary School, Ipswich

Mini-Beasts

I should like to see the wiggly worm in the bumpy dirt,
I should like to hear the rustling leaves when I'm sitting in the tall tree,
I should like to touch the rough bark,
I should like to take home a beautiful butterfly and paint its
                                                colourful wings,
I should like to understand how a slug has a baby.

Conor Sparkes (7)
Rose Hill Primary School, Ipswich

A Woodland Walk

I can see a dark red fox roaming through the undergrowth,
I can see wild rabbits nibbling away at fresh food,
I can see golden-yellow buttercups growing in the grass.

I can feel the cold morning breeze blowing on my face,
I can feel a long, low branch rubbing on my head,
I can feel the leaves crunching under my feet.

I can hear animals calling all around me,
I can hear rustling in the trees
And I can hear blackbirds and sparrows chirping noisily.

Emily Jones (9)
Rose Hill Primary School, Ipswich

A Walk Through The Wood

I can see black ants scurrying next to me,
I can see the ladybirds running on the leaves,
I can feel the long grass tickling on my legs,
I can feel the snails slowly slithering on me,
I can hear birds' wings flapping in the sky,
I can hear my feet crunching on the dead, brown leaves.

Courtney Pattison (9)
Rose Hill Primary School, Ipswich

The Great Forest

I can see a spider carefully spinning a shimmering web
                                    ready to catch his tea,
I can see a woodpecker pecking on the tree,
I can feel the light breeze blowing gently on my face,
I can feel the drip-dropping from the rain on my neck,
I can hear the dead leaves crackling under my feet,
I can hear squirrels scurrying along.

Khyle Phillips (10)
Rose Hill Primary School, Ipswich

Creepy Spiders

A movie muncher
A monster venom injector
A nightmare crasher
A speedy silk web swinger
A creepy-crawlie person frightener
An eight-legged creep
I'm a . . .

Luke Johnson (8)
Rose Hill Primary School, Ipswich

A Funny Animal Poem

A rough rabbit playing rugby
A hideous hare playing hopscotch
A rich rat on roller skates
A handsome hedgehog playing hip hop
A slippery snake playing secret spies
A mini mouse playing massive mania
A feisty fox playing faraway football
A bandaged badger playing bear basketball.

Daniel Garnham (7)
Rose Hill Primary School, Ipswich

Snails

I can see a spiral shell
With different kinds of patterns on it
Shining in the sun.
I can also see a slimy inner skin
All slippery and gooey.

I can feel the wind
Blowing in my face
And the long blades of grass
Skimming my legs.
I can feel the heat of the sun
Against my face.

I can hear the woodpecker
Pecking on my favourite tree
And the grass crunching
Under my feet.

Mahalia Griffin (10)
Rose Hill Primary School, Ipswich

The Wonderful Garden

In the wildlife garden,
I can see a beautiful butterfly fluttering in the sky,
I can see a snail slithering slimily along the path,
I can see a woodlouse crawling out of a piece of bark,
I can see a ladybird crunching on a leaf,
I feel ticklish, like a ladybird is crawling up my arm,
I can feel the wind blowing through my fingers,
I can feel the slime of a snail's trail,
I can feel a money spider climbing up my leg,
I can hear birds humming in the trees,
I can hear a spider hissing like a snake,
I can hear a slug slithering along the path.

Alex Keinzley (9)
Rose Hill Primary School, Ipswich

The Playground Poem

Bendy branches on big brown trees,
Bouncing, soft leaves I see,
Tall, tall trees I see everywhere I go,
Whistles blowing at playtimes and lunch,
Screeching children all around me,
Cracked playgrounds black and grey,
Number snakes and number squares,
Beautiful flowers, purple, blue, yellow, pink,
Hundreds of brown benches,
In lots of places where I like to sit,
Rain falling like soft, white snow,
People drawing on the cracked ground,
People peeping in and out of bushes,
Children chatting, running, skipping,
Playing football, kicking in the goal,
People telling tales.

Jade Nunn (8)
Rose Hill Primary School, Ipswich

Animal Sports I Don't Do

Battling bees batting
Beautiful butterflies bowling
Running rabbits rushing
Funny frogs fielding

Gasping golden eagles gaoling
Slithering snakes striking sensibly
Mad millipedes midfielding
Dancing dragonflies defending

Flying fishes flipping
Bashing bees bouncing.

Jozef Ochwat (7)
Rose Hill Primary School, Ipswich

My Playground

Green, shiny-coated leaves,
Swishing in the breeze.
Rough, bumpy chalk ground,
Stuffed with stones.
Smelly, stinky bins,
Piled with rubbish.
Tall, bendy branches,
Covered with birds.
Smelly lavender,
Grown from seeds.
Crispy, crunchy caterpillars,
Crawl on spiral leaves.
Shrilling whistles from above,
People stopping.
Sticky grass stuck to mud.
The final whistle blows,
Happily, children walk to their lessons.

Luke Howard (9)
Rose Hill Primary School, Ipswich

Snail

I can see a slimy snail slithering along
It looks like it's after a leaf to munch on
With its swirly shell and body of slime
I think a snail is never on time.

I can feel a rock-hard shell
Then I can feel some slimy goo
I think it's quite disgusting
Do you?

I can hear a snail munching on leaves
I can hear a snail slithering across paths
A snail is slow and quiet
So listen carefully to hear it nibbling on the flower petals.

Aidan Bull (9)
Rose Hill Primary School, Ipswich

Senses Of The Maze

I can see,
Trees climbing the invisible ladder to the sky,
Leaves flapping their sails towards me,
Twigs dancing down the path of joy,
Big bumblebees whooshing through leaves.

I can hear,
An aeroplane's engine roaring above my head,
Green leaves flowing in the wind,
Flies buzzing through a natural course,
Birds chirping at their young.

I can feel,
Smooth, green leaves brushing my hair,
Gentle wind pushing on my back,
Soft sand crumbling beneath my feet,
Knobbly twigs poking me gently.

I can smell,
Fresh air circling above my head,
Leaves releasing the smell of nature,
Exhaust fumes in the sky,
Freshness of rain soaking into mud.

Abigail Eaton (10)
Rose Hill Primary School, Ipswich

Down In The Woods

Foxes slinking
Birds flying
Moles digging
Frogs diving
Snakes hunting
Ladybirds scurrying
Spiders building
Slugs feeding.

Benjamin Golding (9)
Rose Hill Primary School, Ipswich

Senses Of The Maze

I can see:
Trees grown tall so the end you cannot see
An insect with striped skin, a vicious bumblebee
A forest ahead of me, full of inspiration
Twigs reaching out to me, or is it my imagination?

I can hear:
Birds in the distance in the trees
Wind rustling the healthy green leaves
Children playing, having a great time
Cars whizzing, ignoring the stop sign.

I can feel:
Smooth, delicate leaves, lying on the ground
The wind in my face that makes no sound
The rough bark that is as strong as a lion
The sun beating down on my head.

I can smell:
The fresh air that smells like the outside
The dust that makes you run and hide
The smell of rosebuds in the air
The pollen floating in my hair.

Emily O'Neill (10)
Rose Hill Primary School, Ipswich

Guess What?

A four-winged, patterned attracter
A crunching, leaf-eating muncher
A whizzing, wise eye-catcher
A clever, changing beautifier
A smooth, long-winged starer
A beautiful, coloured flier,
I'm a . . .

Gianni Lesina (8)
Rose Hill Primary School, Ipswich

Sensing The Maze

What's that I can see?
Leaves on branches, growing, reaching upwards,
Small, grand trees swaying steadily in the crisp breeze,
Rough, brown bark covering the forest floor,
Little white flies busily flitting about.

What's that I can hear?
Chirpy birds cheerfully singing in the air,
The distant rumble of a large plane zooming across the sky,
Busy rushing of cars streaming along the road,
Playful screams from happy children.

What's that I can feel?
Smooth leaves brushing gently against my legs,
Soft sand surrounding my feet,
Sharp plants tugging at my clothes,
Wind rustling leaves and waking up my hair.

What's that I can smell?
Damp piles of rotting leaves,
Warm smells of soft soil,
Cool freshness of clear air,
Sweet smells of opening flower buds.

Jenny Hardwicke (11)
Rose Hill Primary School, Ipswich

Kennings

A frightening room invader
A ferocious venom biter
A black, speedy web spinner
A creepy nightmare maker
A vicious fly muncher
It's a . . .

Jessica Delaney (8)
Rose Hill Primary School, Ipswich

Pupils' Playground

Branches bending on an old sycamore tree,
That's what I see!

Rough leaves, green leaves with red caterpillar eggs,
Leaf stalks look like thin green legs,
That's what I see and feel!

Leaves rustling in the wind,
Whooshing, rustling wind,
That's what I hear!

Brown textured benches,
That's what I feel!

The cracked, hard playground,
That's where I run!

A blue spiral and a red and yellow hopscotch,
That's where I play!

Ellen Wootten (9)
Rose Hill Primary School, Ipswich

My Wonderful Playground

Tall tree rustling,
Brown stalk, green leaves with caterpillar eggs,
Bendy branches,
Rough and bumpy ground
And a blue swirl,
Children running around the playground like racing cars
And giant snakes,
Pupils in the playground
Skipping, running, playing football,
Strong, sweet lavender,
Sharp thistles and seeds
Slowly flying high up into the sky,
Black ants scurrying.

My wonderful playground.

Danielle Fulcher (9)
Rose Hill Primary School, Ipswich

The Playground

Large, old tree, branches swaying
Gracefully side to side.
Green, soft leaves rustling madly.
Shrill whistles quietens children.
This is what I see and hear.
Playground bumpy and cracked.
The great, green snake slithers
Across the playground.
Large number squares
Count up to one hundred.
Textured and tatty old benches
To sit on.
Stinky, smelly bins and drains.
Beautiful flowers painted on the wall.
Luscious lavender smells strong.
Lovely plants, they smell beautiful.
Rain falling from the dark blue sky.
All these things are what I see
In the playground.

Lydia Grant (9)
Rose Hill Primary School, Ipswich

Super Nessie The Dragon

He flies high and far
He flies by sheep and hears the sound *baaa!*
Nessie is the biggest superstar
He always shows off his flashy car.

Nessie has been all over the place
He goes to New York mostly, but all the time he burns his face
He sits at home to watch the athletes race.

His best teddy is red
His day is over, why not go to bed?

Joshua Keeble (10)
Rose Hill Primary School, Ipswich

The School Environment Poem

Cheerful children chase around,
Happy girls walk and talk,
You can hear loud and noisy voices,
In the maze, children have some fun,
Trains go by as children run,
At 1.00pm there's a whistle that is deafening,
Some children drop an earring,
From loud to silent when third whistle blows,
Children line up in rows,
Look carefully when there's peace,
First you see nothing,
Then they crawl up to you,
Scurrying ants and beetles,
Slimy snails and wriggly worms,
No humans now, but as busy as ever.

Callum Sparkes (9)
Rose Hill Primary School, Ipswich

The Playground Poem

Big, old, tatty tree,
Hear the rustling of the large overlapping leaves,
Small, red caterpillar eggs sitting on the leaves,
Number snake swerving across the playground,
Small, cracked chain laying in the middle of the playground,
Silver water fountains to quench our thirst,
No green grass to play on!
Lovely, long purple irises by an old bench,
Lots and lots of wooden features,
Giant painted flowers on the wall,
Big, long, green leaves,
Lots of tiny creatures,
Tiny potato houses with swarms of ants in,
Smells of lavender and blossom trees swaying in the wind,
A small corner of tree bark with ants and ladybirds in it,
This is why my playground is great!

Ellie Sampson (8)
Rose Hill Primary School, Ipswich

Poor Old Lucy Mayne

Poor old Lucy Mayne
Stomped through the windy rain
Her hair was tied in a greasy bow
Which said quite faintly 'Fun and co.'

Her knees were bruised
Her arms were weak
Her eyes were small
Her nose like a beak.

She lived in a flat
With her mum and her cat
The only good thing
Was the bathroom mat.

Her rundown car
Was rusty red
Her bedroom was awful
With a small bed.

Emily Kenny (10)
Rose Hill Primary School, Ipswich

Animals

A nimals arrive to eat apples
B ouncing bugs bounce to get the bananas first
C lever, crazy cats call themselves Chloe
D ancing, diving ducks dance on the ice
E dible elephants enjoy eating eggs
F unny frogs find hunting flies hard
G rimy, green grasshoppers like to eat great spiders
H airy horses hate hairy hogs.

Nichola Sapsed (10)
Rose Hill Primary School, Ipswich

Sensors In The Maze

I can see greens, piles of leaves,
Autumn colours all around,
A miniature forest!
Chocolate coloured bark and soil!

I can hear tiny birds chirping,
Tweet, tweet, the blackbirds sing,
Microscopic flies buzzing around me,
At night it will be silent.

I can feel smooth leaves,
Rough bark and bumpy stones,
Some leaves silky, some leaves furry,
I feel happy.

I can't smell much . . .
Fresh air is all around me,
The smell of it makes me tingle inside,
I love the smell of fresh air.

Madison Nunn (11)
Rose Hill Primary School, Ipswich

Butterfly

I fly above you every day
How beautiful I hear you say
At night I sleep, at day I play
My beautiful wings come out today
My antennae look out for prey
I think I'll say I really need to play
On breathtaking flowers I will always stay.

Alexandra Kell (11)
Rose Hill Primary School, Ipswich

Tragic Wars

Dry saliva trickling down my lumpy throat
The disgusting aftertaste of last night's supper.

Empathy rushing through me
Tortuous thoughts destroying me
My heart pounding and racing
Devastating destruction!

The wind blowing rapidly and fiercely
Shooting of tormenting shotguns
Old muddy boots stomping and marching.

Pouring, running and dripping blood
Grass gently swaying in the wind
Intimidated soldiers dying painfully
Tears falling from desolated families.

Bethany Exworth (10)
Rose Hill Primary School, Ipswich

My Magic Box
(Inspired by 'Magic Box' by Kit Wright)

I'd put in my box . . .
Ten thousand wishes of pure golden rays
Over and over again.

I'd put in my box . . .
All my memories with friends
Then I would never forget them.

I'd put in my box . . .
A dream I had not dreamt
And a black limo with special coloured numbers.

I'd use my box . . .
To fly it like a dragon that could breathe fire
And that burned enemies to ashes.

Timothy Florax (10)
Rudham CE Primary School, King's Lynn

Seaside Sounds

We are the pebbles that
Ratter and tatter, ratter and tatter.

We are the waves that
Splish and splash, splish and splash.

We are the seagulls that
Eek and ack, eek and ack.

We are the waves that
Splish and splash, splish and splash.

We are the fish that
Oop and app, oop and app.

We are the waves that
Splish and splash, splish and splash.

We are the boats that
Bib and bob, bib and bob.

Charlotte Maloney Parr-Burman (6)
Rudham CE Primary School, King's Lynn

Where Do All The Teachers Go?

Where do all the teachers go
When it's four o'clock?
Do they go and boogie?
Do they wear sun block?

Do they wear pyjamas?
Do they watch TV?
Do they ever get cross?
Do they ever get stung by a bee?

I'll follow one back home today
I'll find out what they do
Then I'll put it in a poem
Then they can read it to you.

Archie Cross (7)
Rudham CE Primary School, King's Lynn

Where Do All The Teachers Go?

Where do all the teachers go
When it is four o'clock?
Do they drive a car
Or do they wash their socks?

Do they eat spaghetti?
Do they go to discos?
Do they go for walks?
Do they watch videos?

Do they wear pyjamas?
Do they play ball?
Do they watch TV?
Or do they walk the hall?

Do they eat bananas?
Do they climb trees?
Do they do handstands?
Or do they catch bees?

Danielle Meyern (8)
Rudham CE Primary School, King's Lynn

Where Do All The Teachers Go?

Where do all the teachers go
When it's four o'clock?
They go into the drawers
Looking for an old sock.

Do they ever clean their teeth?
Have they ever crashed their cars?
Do they ever wash their feet?
Do they jump over crossbars?

Do they ever wear their shoes?
Have they ever had a bath?
Did they ever cry when they lost their dogs?
Did they ever milk a calf?

Bradley White (8)
Rudham CE Primary School, King's Lynn

Where Do All The Teachers Go?

Where do all the teachers go
When it's four o'clock?
Do they go to the disco
To dance and jive and rock?

Do they dress in normal clothes
And do they have a wife?
Have they liked sweets and chocolate
All the way through their life?

Did they have a dog or cat
And did they feed them well?
Did they nag their mums and ask
To ring the village bell?

Do they play an instrument,
A guitar, or bass or cello?
Do they consider what they wear
In the colour blue or yellow?

I think about my teachers
And what they're supposed to do
And I wonder if when they're at home
They think of me and you!

Eleanor Maloney Parr-Burman (8)
Rudham CE Primary School, King's Lynn

I Will Put In The Box . . .

(Inspired by 'Magic Box' by Kit Wright)

I will put in the box . . .
A multicoloured football
A teddy bear as big as a tree
A Barbie doll as pink as pink.

I will put in the box . . .
Some money that's fallen from the sky
And a monkey that has come from space.

Holly Page (10)
Rudham CE Primary School, King's Lynn

Where Do All The Teachers Go?

Where do all the teachers go
When it's 4 o'clock?
Do they go to a disco
To rock, rock, rock?

Do they wear pyjamas
And do they watch TV?
Do people watch them
When they go for a wee?

Do they live with other people?
Have they mums and dads?
Are they always happy
Or are they always sad?

Do they go out in town
Or do they go to The Crown?
Do they go to the Cat and Fiddle
Or do they sing a riddle?

Heather McKinnon (9)
Rudham CE Primary School, King's Lynn

I Will Put In My Box . . .
(Inspired by 'Magic Box' by Kit Wright)

I will put in my box . . .
A dinosaur with sparkly teeth
And eyes that shine in the sunny breeze,
That runs like the wind
And feels like a soft blanket
That's just come out of the washing machine.

I will put in my box . . .
A butterfly with wings like sparkly gold
And flies like the wind.

Cally Haclin (9)
Rudham CE Primary School, King's Lynn

Where Do All The Teachers Go?

Where do all the teachers go
When it's four o'clock?
Do they go to the beach
And put on sun block?

Do they get ill
And do they get chickenpox?
And did they used to eat
From a lunch box?

Did they used to write neatly?
Did they flip a coin?
Do they eat meat
From a beef sirloin?

Did they ever kick soil?
Did they ever jump like a frog?
Did they ever gargle
And did they ever have a lame dog?

Did they ever go on holiday?
Did they ever wish?
Did they ever do a quiz?
Did they like starfish?

I'll follow one back home today
I'll find out what they do
Then I'll put it in a poem
That they can read to you.

Luke Henson (9)
Rudham CE Primary School, King's Lynn

Where Do All The Teachers Go?

Where do all the teachers go
After four o'clock?
Do they work on a farm
And count their flock?

Do they go roller skating
And have some fun?
Or go to a shop
And get an iced bun?

Do they go to a fancy dress
Or play a part in a play?
Or do they run away
Straight away?

Do they go to play
Or go for an X-ray
Down the alleyway?
Let's go Saturday.

I'll follow one back home today
I'll find out what they do
Then I'll put it in a poem
That they can tell you.

Georgina Meyern (9)
Rudham CE Primary School, King's Lynn

Emotion
(Inspired by 'Pied Piper' by Robert Browning)

Shining in the sun
That burns on my forehead
I heard sweet music ring
In my head I hear it sing.
Run from my life
The worry and strife
I want to turn my back
But what I lack
Is far from my fears.

I am thirsty
My energy drained
What I am missing cannot be gained.
Stumbling, reaching
Straining, yearning
I break down
Beating the ground
I mustn't look back
I move on.

My head turns
I close my eyes
I can't face the lies.
I stare at the fire
All my desire
Ebbing away
Into the ashes
Two words in my mind
As I stare behind
I lost.

Josie Henson (11)
Rudham CE Primary School, King's Lynn

Seaside Sounds

We are the shells
That go clang and clash,
Clang and clash,
Clang and clash.

We are the breeze
That goes blow and whoosh,
Blow and whoosh,
Blow and whoosh.

We are the sea
That goes swish and bash,
Swish and bash,
Swish and bash.

We are the breeze
That goes blow and whoosh,
Blow and whoosh,
Blow and whoosh.

We are the waves
That roll and tumble,
Roll and tumble,
Roll and tumble.

We are the breeze
That goes blow and whoosh,
Blow and whoosh,
Blow and whoosh.

Michaela Pitkin-Bovington (9)
Rudham CE Primary School, King's Lynn

The Magic Box
(Inspired by 'Magic Box' by Kit Wright)

I will put in my box . . .
The sun setting slowly
Over a field of golden-brown corn,
A bottle of turquoise water
From the glimmering lake,
A ruby made by an *exploding* wish.

I will put in my box . . .
A fierce flash of lightning
From the Greek god Zeus,
The sensation of crisp-white snowflakes
Falling gently on my stone-cold fingers.

I will put in my box . . .
A glittering star
Dangling down on an invisible thread,
Sherlock Holmes' magnifying glass,
A flying pig in a pink tutu,
Who says pigs can't fly?

Lizzie Prentis (11)
Rudham CE Primary School, King's Lynn

I Will Put In My Box . . .
(Inspired by 'Magic Box' by Kit Wright)

I will put in my box . . .
A jar of fresh air from Mount Everest,
A jug of water from the Angel Falls,
Ten glistening rubies from a Chinese dragon.

I will put in my box . . .
Warm, mouth-watering chocolate
From Willy Wonka's factory,
The morning birds tweeting a calm, soothing song,
A wish from the bottom of my heart.

Jamie Thompson (11)
Rudham CE Primary School, King's Lynn

Seaside Sounds

We are the children that shout and scream,
Shout and scream.
We are the seagulls that peck,
Peck, peck.
We are the fish that splish, splash, splosh,
Splish, splash, splosh.
We are the seagulls that peck,
Peck, peck.
We are the boats that bib and bob,
Bib and bob.
We are the seagulls that peck,
Peck, peck.
We are the dogs that bark and run,
Bark and run.
We are the seagulls that peck,
Peck, peck.

Thomas Hill (8)
Rudham CE Primary School, King's Lynn

Where Do All The Teachers Go?

Where do all the teachers go
When it's four o'clock?
Do they go to discos to rock, rock, rock?

Where do all the teachers go
When it's four o'clock?
Do they go to hospital to see their mates
Or do they bake cakes?

Next time when I go home
I will follow one home
And see what they do
And put it in a poem.

Fleur Murphy (8)
Rudham CE Primary School, King's Lynn

I Will Put In My Box . . .
(Inspired by 'Magic Box' by Kit Wright)

I will put in my box . . .
A glowing, shooting star
A rock from the middle of each planet
A sapphire caused by an exploding wish.

I will put in my box . . .
A scary monster with a big mouth
A big dragon that circles the moon
A puff of the coldest air.

I will put in my box . . .
An alien big and green
An enchanted beast created by my mind
A darting fish leaving a golden trail.

I will put in the box . . .
A magical leaf which grants all wishes
A skull of a golden snake which rattles in the wind
A raging stream of water from the highest mountain.

Jack McCarthy (10)
Rudham CE Primary School, King's Lynn

Socks

S melly socks, scented socks
O n a drying rack
C atching the rays of the sun
K illing damp on their back
S melly socks, scented socks.

Ryan Hatton (10)
St Margaret's CE Primary School, Halstead

Playtimes At School

The playtimes we have at our school
Are full of children being fools.
Children from four to eleven
Think of this time as heaven.

Screaming and shouting you can hear
You don't need to be standing near.
Running of feet is also heard
You can't hear the sound of a bird.

If you look around you will see
The moving mouths of you and me.
Another sight that could catch your eye
Would be the fast feet charging by.

The playtimes we have at our school
Are full of children being fools.
Children from four to eleven
Think of this time as heaven.

Hannah Pyman (10)
St Margaret's CE Primary School, Halstead

Girls And Boys

Girls like blue and pink
Boys mess around with ink

Girls enjoy shopping
But boys hate mopping

Girls wash and blink
While boys smell and stink

Boys like dogs and cats
Girls are revising for their SATs!

Connie James (11)
St Margaret's CE Primary School, Halstead

Would You Care?

Would you care
If I fell through the air
And landed with a thud on the ground?

Would you look
When an evil cook
Took me for a stew?

Would you throw a rope
When I couldn't cope
At the moment that I drowned?

Would you be a friend
And maybe lend
Something for me to do?

Would you care
If I fell through the air
And landed with a thud on the ground?

Sasha Osborn (10)
St Margaret's CE Primary School, Halstead

A Town Poem

Children play in the playground,
Dogs bark in the compound.
Cats roam in the misty street,
The elderly fall asleep in the warm seat,
The lights glitter in the moonlight.
Everything goes black,
Until the sunlight comes back.

Iszak Smith (9)
St Margaret's CE Primary School, Halstead

Families

Without my family I could not live,
My heart would be like a giant sieve.

Without any family where would you be?
Under the ground or up a tree.

Families give you support and love,
The friendship between you is high above.

They give you chocolates and pets,
But sometimes they slip into debts.

When you're in trouble they will always be there,
Because they will always take good care.

Without my family I could not live,
My heart would be like a giant sieve.

Amelia Quinn (11)
St Margaret's CE Primary School, Halstead

Eyes

Eyes all different
In all sorts of ways,
Eyes that sparkle
When you gaze.
Eyes to look
And see your friends,
Eyes are different
In all sorts of ways!

Lauren Platt (9)
St Margaret's CE Primary School, Halstead

Portrait Of Queen Elizabeth I

There was a young girl,
Who had been in prison,
Elizabeth was her name,
Finally came out of prison,
She was free at last.

One day she sat under a tree
Reading a book,
A tall man came up to her,
'Mary is dead,' he said and gave her the ring,
At last the time had come to become Queen.

Her coronation took ten hours,
Her hair was drooping down,
It was here at last,
Her face was white as paper,
With her lovely frock.

Her wig was jewelled with pearls and rubies,
The pearls were her favourite,
The ears and eyes meant she knew everything.

She brought England out from the darkness,
Her frocks were worth half a million pounds,
Her crown was going slowly
And death had overtaken her.

Farwa Jeddy (10)
St Philip's Priory School, Chelmsford

Butterfly

A butterfly is like a sapphire blue petrol floating
Flapping gently like a beautiful fairy
Her eyes like ten thousand diamonds
As she jumps from flower to flower
Sucking the nectar from flowers
Then she flutters into the sky so high
As she draws attention to everything around her
Everything she goes past awakens and blooms.

Alexander Read (8)
St Philip's Priory School, Chelmsford

Portrait Of Queen Elizabeth I

Princess Elizabeth, though not Queen,
Was very rich in portraits,
She always wore pearls
And rings and more.

Elizabeth became Queen in 1558,
Her frock of gold with jewels,
Her hair flowed down,
And with the crown,
She looked so beautiful.

As Queen she reigned,
With feather and fan,
Her face so serious too.

Her hands so slender,
Looked great with the ring,
That gave her all the power.

Her spies are around,
With their ears and eyes,
Watching and hearing everything you do.

Sick with pneumonia,
Last year on the throne to come
And dying in 1603.

Elysia Booker (10)
St Philip's Priory School, Chelmsford

Butterfly

A butterfly is like a pink rose tinged with purple lilac
Flapping in a sapphire blue sky
She jumps from rose to iris
Happily drinking nectar with her long straw tongue
She gracefully flies past people making them smile
She shows her beautiful wings to other insects
Making them look as pretty as possible
Soaring in the air like an elegant feather, floating slowly.

Samuel Taylor Burns (8)
St Philip's Priory School, Chelmsford

Mystery Poem

In a place
Where no one seems to live,
But unknown people roam the street
That no one wants to meet.

Where they live,
Everything you can see,
The lights on the streets,
The lights inside building after building,
Work like the bulb's been changed.
But nothing is seen of the people,
Who live in this unusual scene.

In this place of strange beings,
There aren't any creatures or natural growth,
Such as cats, dogs and trees,
Not even a fly hovers in the air,
Or a weed, a flower, refreshing this place.
When you look in its mists,
You are forgotten and never seen again.

Edward Lakin (10)
St Philip's Priory School, Chelmsford

A Butterfly

A butterfly is like a breeze

B e like the wind, butterfly
U p into the sky
T he colours on her are like a rainbow
T he wind makes her prance and dance
E very time she lands, she greedily sips the nectar
R adiantly her body shines in the sunshine
F luttering as she goes
L eaving a flower behind again
Y ou must be amazed by the butterfly.

Cara Chan (8)
St Philip's Priory School, Chelmsford

The Strange Girl

A girl lives down the lane
Down my lane
She goes to my school
She's in my class

She's got a few friends in our class
But never invites them round
We never see her mum
Nor her dad

One day I walked her home
We arrived, said bye
I turned round and as I looked back
I saw her run down the road where the houses are really bad

I realised
That she was a liar
As we ate our nosh
I told everyone she wasn't posh.

Chengetai Chirewa (10)
St Philip's Priory School, Chelmsford

Butterfly

A butterfly is like a cloud floating by,
Her wings as red as blood and as blue as a sapphire,
She flies from flower to flower sipping with her hollow tongue,
With colours and pretty patterns all over her body,
She jumps and spreads her wings with ruby-red wings,
A butterfly is as pretty as a thousand diamonds,
She flaps her wings so gently and sparkles in the sunshine,
She is a delicate, delicate treasure,
When you see a butterfly, she puts a smile on your face,
As she waits for the flowers to open in the spring.

Max Purkiss (8)
St Philip's Priory School, Chelmsford

The Portraits Of Queen Elizabeth

It all started when her sister died,
How thrilled she was to hear,
She was queen of England,
Her powerful reign started here.

In her ten-hour coronation,
She waited silently,
In her beautiful gold dress,
Encrusted with jewels,
Crown on her head,
Beautiful cloak on her shoulders
And a very serious look on her face.

In her beautiful white dress,
Dotted with precious stones,
Jewels galore
And her waist so thin.

Queen Elizabeth was ill,
Death was lurking near,
She was ready to go,
Her people were very sad,
The cherubs removing the crown,
Off her thin hair.

Hester Catchpole (10)
St Philip's Priory School, Chelmsford

Butterfly

A butterfly is like the green of the leaves
She has sparkly wings as she flies from flower to flower
She floats like a smooth feather floating
She flies silently, she is so quiet
She is quite like a crystal
Her wings feel like tissue paper
She twinkles in the sun, she is a graceful butterfly
She is fluttering her wings
Her eyes are as blue as the sky.

Maham Qureshi (8)
St Philip's Priory School, Chelmsford

Portrait Of Queen Elizabeth

A strong queen of England
Stood ambitiously tall and proud
Hundreds of years ago
Her hair creeping down her back

At her coronation
Leaving her hair free to disperse
Determined to learn in her youth
Struggling England through eras

Her exuberant and powerful reign
Made England a greatly prosperous country
A skilled queen of England
Who will never be forgotten

She resolutely took the responsibility
Of ruling England
And fought off
One of the greatest fleets ever

In her last days
She awaited death
She could see all and hear all
Hundreds of years ago.

Sam Purkiss (10)
St Philip's Priory School, Chelmsford

Butterfly

A butterfly is like a red, red rose,
Her wings are like tissue paper floating,
She is as graceful as a ballerina,
Her eyes are like crystals,
Her body twinkles in the sunshine,
The meadows have her favourite flowers,
Her antennae sway in the air,
It makes me smile when I see her beauty.

Megan Larner-Hoskins (8)
St Philip's Priory School, Chelmsford

The Last Supper

It was a dark, wistful night,
My last meal with my master,
I could feel his excruciating sadness,
His life almost at an end,
Down to one treacherous man, Judas.

His words were clear, but could not be understood,
He knelt down and washed our feet, I was shocked.
'I would die for you,' he said,
At that I was perplexed,
I don't want him to die.

He broke the bread and said, 'This is my body,'
Then shared out the wine, 'This is my blood.'
I looked at Judas' empty chair,
My heart was filled with anger.

I had never hurt so much,
I was lost and distraught,
This meal was,
The Last Supper.

Rosanna Beaver (9)
St Philip's Priory School, Chelmsford

Light Haikus

When the sun rises,
Bright and gleaming in the sky,
Waking up the earth.

Bright and gleaming now,
In the middle of the day,
Singing joyfully.

The sun is setting,
With beautiful colours
Surrounding itself.

Erin Lucid (9)
St Philip's Priory School, Chelmsford

A Mystery Poem

What was that?
There were creaks among the floorboards,
Whisper sounds, what were they?
Wait, I heard another movement,
A footstep moving extremely slowly,
Wandering around my house.

Shall we take a risk?
Go and see what it is?
A swish of air moving about our heads,
Was that Mum upstairs?
No, she was out.
What about Dad?
He was at work.

I'll go and see who it is,
But I will have to be quiet.
I went upstairs,
Slithering as slow as a snake.

I saw something move,
A swish of hair
Moving just past me,
Didn't see me.

She had a pointy nose,
Just like my gran,
But horrible hair and wicked teeth,
Chattering away.

I was so scared,
Puzzled as anything.
Voices, movements, what next?
Waiting to be found.

Sophie Lampshire (10)
St Philip's Priory School, Chelmsford

Portrait Of Queen Elizabeth

Queen Mary the Catholic,
Had come to the end of her life,
The moment she had been dreading,
And then died 402 years ago.

The ring had been handed over to Elizabeth,
Who put it finally on her finger,
Hail to Queen Elizabeth,
Because she is now queen.

In the middle portrait,
She is now crowned to be queen,
In the one next to it she is dying,
The one above it is her,
A year before she died from a disease.

The one next to it is
When she was very serious
And she was wearing the crown
And nobody could take it from her.

Below that portrait
Is one where she
Is standing in England
And just maybe in Oxfordshire,
Behind her she is standing in the light,
It represents that she is
Leading England out of misery
And into the new world.

Nadia Wheadon (10)
St Philip's Priory School, Chelmsford

Portrait Of Queen Elizabeth

Her coronation portrait
An early portrait of her
Her garment rich and superior,
The sceptre in her hand.

The portrait of sun and storm
She brings us to the light of sun,
From all stormy days and nights
On the land of Oxfordshire.

The portrait of all eyes and ears,
Her spies are everywhere,
Always watching, always listening
So don't plot against her.

The portrait of the Armada,
The English fleet are victorious,
The globe is in her hand,
She rules it all, so stay away.

The portrait of power,
The feathers are a rarity,
She got the crown,
So don't plot!

The portrait of life and death,
Death is interested in her,
Her crown is taken,
But she will die in power.

Hallam Dyckhoff (10)
St Philip's Priory School, Chelmsford

Elizabeth I

Elizabeth was a clever woman,
Her favourite jewels were pearls,
She didn't marry,
Her coronation picture
Was when she was just a queen.

As she sits upon the throne,
She can hear and see,
Her portrait is very rich
And shines a lot with anger.

On her rainbow picture,
She is dying,
How very tired she is
And very near death.

She is brave and powerful,
She is very tired,
She can't tell,
Or she will be weak.
She is very wise,
She won't be taken as a fool,
She looks very tired
And very scared.

Elena Impieri (10)
St Philip's Priory School, Chelmsford

Butterfly

A butterfly is like a darting flower,
With ruby and sapphire-coloured wings,
Her eyes are ten thousand diamonds
And her long tongue sips nectar from her favourite flower.
The queen of the meadows,
She is a piece of glitter in the sky,
Shines like the princess of all the insects,
With her antennae twitching.

Will Adams (8)
St Philip's Priory School, Chelmsford

Portrait Of Queen Elizabeth I

In the portrait of her coronation,
Her dazzling, golden hair let loose
And her crown placed on top,
With her big jewels scattered
All over her expensive dress.

Forty-five years later,
In the portrait of her death,
The skeleton of death
Has come to take her away,
While the angel of death
Is taking her crown away.

In the portrait of war,
Between danger and safety,
She is leaving danger behind
And leading us to safety,
While stepping on England!

Queen Elizabeth loved jewels,
Expensive jewels,
She wore them in her hair
And all over her gowns
And she had a boyfriend!

Ridhae Sheikh (10)
St Philip's Priory School, Chelmsford

Butterfly

A butterfly is as beautiful as a crystal,
A butterfly has shiny eyes,
A butterfly's wings are as lovely as a diamond,
A butterfly is like a fern,
A butterfly flutters in the air,
A butterfly floats on the wind,
A butterfly is lovely,
A butterfly is wonderful.

Francesca Impieri (8)
St Philip's Priory School, Chelmsford

School Days

Going to bed at half-past eight
When there's things you want to watch on the telly
Marching up those horrible stairs
Grumpy and tired

You get in the bath
And wash with soap
Wash your hair
Then dry off

You get your jim-jams on
Turn the light off
Get into bed
And go to sleep

Ding, ding, ding
There goes the alarm
The clock says half-past seven
You turn it off and go to sleep again

Half an hour later
Wake up please
With a great big sneeze
In comes the mum

You get up and get dressed
Have your breakfast
Get in the car
Off you go

Get out of the car
Give your mum a kiss
Get into school
Hand your homework in
The bell goes

    And there goes another
    Hard day at school.

Sam Davis (10)
St Philip's Priory School, Chelmsford

Circus

Paint flying everywhere
One ordinary old lady
Everybody laughing at the clowns
Mothers shouting with delight
Seals performing on their stands

Atmosphere roaring to get out
Ringmaster calling for silence
Eager children ready for action

Tightrope walker steadily going
Happy bears dancing around
Elephants parading round the ring

Beastly lions frightening children
Excited performers all nervous
Stilts clanking on the floor
The rabbit comes out of the hat

Bare, nothing like before
You and me saying goodbye
Everybody has gone home.

Danielle Tinloi (10)
St Philip's Priory School, Chelmsford

Butterfly

A butterfly is like a gentle feather,
Her colours are as blue as the sky,
With ruby-red rings on her wings,
She jumps from flower to flower,
Her eyes are like ten thousand diamonds,
Her antennae are twitching in the wind,
She makes people smile going by,
She is prettier than the flowers she's on,
She is the queen of all butterflies.

Katie Lampshire (8)
St Philip's Priory School, Chelmsford

The Castle

'Your room is on the fourth floor,
Sixth room on the left,'
Said Martin's mother,
'And don't get lost.'

'As if I would get lost,'
Said Martin,
On the second floor.
'Oh, you will get lost,'
Said a voice behind a door.

Martin was frightened,
'Mum!' he yelled.
Silence, then the voice said again,
'Oh yes, I knew you would get lost.'

At this Martin felt brave,
He barged into the room,
And then . . .

Jessica Jellicoe (10)
St Philip's Priory School, Chelmsford

Butterfly

A butterfly is like the queen of the fairies,
She floats gracefully,
She has eyes shining like ten thousand diamonds,
Her wings sparkling in the light,
She flutters in the breeze,
Her wings as purple as lavender,
She sucks the nectar,
Her legs as thin as a hair.

Francesca Read (8)
St Philip's Priory School, Chelmsford

Butterfly

A butterfly is like a cloud floating in the sky,
She trips from flower to flower,
Her wings are like feathers floating from side to side,
Her eyes like crystals,
She shines like the sunlight,
She is as pretty as a princess,
She moves like a little ballerina,
She's the queen of all fairies.

Nelia Leong (8)
St Philip's Priory School, Chelmsford

Leaves

Leaves are green,
Sometimes a little yellow.
Crack, crack,
Cracking like an Easter egg broken off.
When I took it away,
It was windy, windy, very windy.
It flew up high and whizzed around,
Up and down,
Round and round,
Like a runaway train,
Landing in some deep chocolate mud.
Then it walked over to the blossom tree,
She watched the leaves,
Stayed like a statue for months, days,
Until her August confetti fell down.

Vanessa Allen (7)
Salhouse Primary School, Norwich

My Flower

Went outside,
Went for a walk,
Rose-pink flower cracked,
Now it's gone.
Heart is broken,
Don't know what to do,
Stroked it gently,
Felt the silk.

Sophie Thurling (7)
Salhouse Primary School, Norwich

Mysterious Flower

Walked along a sunny field,
Yellow flower waving,
Picked with a careful pinch,
Disappeared forever.

Grady Patten (7)
Salhouse Primary School, Norwich

Butterfly

The multicoloured butterfly slowly and silently swoops down
To a tulip that is calling him.
As the master of the sky gets to the tulip,
He gently sky-walks to the tulip to rest.
He does not know where he's going next,
But he knows he has but a little time to live.

Sarah Papworth (11)
Tilney St Lawrence CP School, Tilney St Lawrence

Season Meanings

Summer includes
Sun, sea, sand.
Winter includes
Frozen land.
Autumn includes
Leaves falling.
Spring includes
Blossom calling.

Helena Bonici (11)
Westwood Primary School, Benfleet

Dog Kennings

A water drinker
A tail chaser
A biscuit eater
A ball catcher
A stick fetcher
A cat fighter
A cool walker
That makes me a dog!

Thomas Haylock (8)
Westwood Primary School, Benfleet

A Snake Kennings

A slimy slitherer,
A venom spitter,
A small hisser,
A frozen rat eater,
A disgusting swallower,
A poison spitter,
A hard biter,
Apple eater,
Snake!

Thomas Clubb (8)
Westwood Primary School, Benfleet

The Night Everyone Fears

You're standing by the roaring sea,
It's colder than the coldest tea,
Like a fist pounding against the coastline,
You'd be mad to say that this is fine,
You are standing in a thunderous storm,
You're pouring with sweat, very warm.

You smell oil from smashed oil tanks,
You'd be a wally to say thanks,
This is raging and unstoppable,
Slicing down the great town hall,
It sounds like an alien theme,
'What?' you say, 'Is this a dream?'

The waves are mountainous,
The coastline, you and I are defenceless,
Look! Look over there,
The sea is like a great bear,
This really is not good now,
Whoa! Watch out! *Pow!*

Andrew Brown (11)
Westwood Primary School, Benfleet

Olympics

The Olympics is a great competition,
To win gold is an athlete's mission.

800m and the long jump,
Injuries from a broken leg to a small bump.

Bronze, silver and gold,
All contestants have to be strong and bold.

I want to be an athlete when I'm older,
But first I have to finish my geography folder!

George Hughes (10)
Westwood Primary School, Benfleet

A Nature Trail

Leaves on trees
Buzzing bees
I smell the grass
And sparrows pass.

The flowers sway in the breeze
The pollen makes me sneeze
Pond animals, bugs and frogs
I can also see big fat logs.

Clouds in the sky
Dragonflies whizz by
In fields there are mice and rats
Hanging from trees I see bats.

Leaves on trees
Buzzing bees
I smell the grass
As sparrows pass.

Chloe Harman (10)
Westwood Primary School, Benfleet

A Caterpillar

A caterpillar crawls and crawls
As he moves along the ground
And then he sits amongst the leaves
And once he spins a chrysalis
A butterfly comes out.

A butterfly flies and flies
Then sits amongst the leaves
He lays his eggs
Then finally caterpillars
Are again.

Heather Wilson (9)
Westwood Primary School, Benfleet